WOODROW WILSON

THE FORUM OF
DEMOCRACY

BY

DWIGHT EVERETT WATKINS

PROFESSOR OF PUBLIC SPEAKING
KNOX COLLEGE, GALESBURG, ILLINOIS

AND

ROBERT EDWARD WILLIAMS

INSTRUCTOR IN PUBLIC SPEAKING
KNOX COLLEGE

*Government of the people, by the people,
and for the people, shall not perish from
the earth.*
— LINCOLN.

ALLYN AND BACON
Boston   New York   Chicago

Norwood Press
J. S. Cushing Co. — Berwick & Smith Co.
Norwood, Mass., U.S.A.

PREFACE

THE aim of this book is to inspire patriotism, to set forth the democratic ideals of the United States and its associates in the Great War, and at the same time to furnish classes in reading and speaking with a new, interesting, and stimulating collection of the writings and speeches of the master minds of to-day.

Not only are these selections valuable for reading and for study, they are filled with a dramatic appeal and an intensity of feeling and purpose which make them especially suited to classes in declamation.

Men feel deeply, think earnestly, and speak sincerely in times of tragic crisis. Under these conditions oratory flourishes. Such was the case in 1775, when Patrick Henry, James Otis, and others called down the wrath of the people of the new world on the tyranny of the old; such was the case in '61 and the white-hot years preceding, when Calhoun and Webster, Beecher and Lincoln set forth the conflicting views on slavery and union.

To-day, as in the past, men's truest thoughts and highest aspirations are being given to the world by her great statesmen and thinkers. Out of this furnace-heat of conflict thoughts have been given expression, ideals voiced, and convictions stated, so forceful in character and so beautiful in form that they deserve a permanent place in the literature of coming generations.

The sources have been many and varied. British pamphlets, the Bulletin of the Paris Chamber of Commerce, and the newspaper reports to the United States have been freely drawn upon. Especially valuable has been the assistance of the *New York Times Current History Magazine,* without whose kind permission to reprint various copyrighted extracts this little volume would have been impossible.

D. E. W.
R. E. W.

Novermber, 1917.

TABLE OF CONTENTS

LIST OF ILLUSTRATIONS

THE FORUM OF DEMOCRACY

THE FORUM OF DEMOCRACY

ENGLAND UNSHEATHES THE SWORD

Premier Asquith

My Lord Mayor and Citizens of London: It is three and a half years since I last had the honor of addressing in this hall a gathering of the citizens. We were then met under the Presidency of one of your predecessors, men of all creeds and parties, to celebrate and approve the joint declaration of the two great English-speaking States that for the future any differences between them should be settled, if not by agreement, at least by judicial inquiry and arbitration, and never in any circumstances by war. Those of us who hailed that great Eirenicon between the United States and ourselves as a landmark on the road of progress were not sanguine enough to think, or even to hope, that the era of war was drawing to a close. But still less were we prepared to anticipate the terrible spectacle which now confronts us of a contest which for the number and importance of the powers

---

On September 5, 1914, soon after the outbreak of the war, Prime Minister Asquith addressed a great body of people at the Guildhall in London.

The Right Honorable Herbert Henry Asquith was born at Morley, Yorkshire, in 1852 and was educated at the City of London School and at Balliol College, Oxford. Mr. Asquith had held many high offices in the gift of the British nation before he became Prime Minister in 1908. He was superseded in this office by David Lloyd George in January of 1917.

engaged, the scale of their armaments and armies, the width of the theater of conflict, the outpouring of blood and the loss of life, the incalculable toll of suffering levied upon non-combatants, the material and moral loss accumulating day by day to the higher interests of civilized mankind — a contest which in every one of these aspects is without precedent in the annals of the world. We were very confident three years ago in the rightness of our position, when we welcomed the new securities for peace. We are equally confident in it today, when reluctantly, and against our will, but with a clear judgment and a clean conscience we find ourselves involved with the whole strength of this empire in a bloody arbitration between might and right. The issue has passed out of the domain of argument into another field, but let me ask you, and through you the world outside, what would have been our condition as a nation to-day if we had been base enough through timidity or through perverted calculation of self-interest, or through a paralysis of the sense of honor and duty (cheers), if we had been base enough to be false to our word and faithless to our friends?

Our eyes would have been turned at this moment with those of the whole civilized world to Belgium, a small State, which has lived for more than seventy years under the several and collective guarantee to which we in common with Prussia and Austria were parties, and we should have seen at the instance and by the action of two of these guaranteeing powers her neutrality violated, her independence strangled, her territory made use of as affording the easiest and the most convenient road to a war of unprovoked aggression against France. We, the British people, would at this moment have been standing by with folded arms and with such countenance as we could command while this small and unprotected State, in defense of her vital liberties, made a heroic stand against over-weening and overwhelming force; we should have been admiring as detached spectators the siege of Liége, the steady and manful resistance of a small army to the occupation of their capital, with its splendid traditions and memories, the gradual forcing back of the patriotic defenders of their native land to the ramparts of Antwerp, countless outrages inflicted by buccaneering levies exacted from the unoffending civil population, and, finally, the greatest crime committed against civilization and culture since the Thirty Years' War, the sack of Louvain, with its buildings, its pictures, its unique library, its unrivaled associations — a shameless holocaust of irreparable treasures lit up by blind barbarian vengeance. What account should we, the Government and the people of this country, have been able to render to the tribunal of our national conscience and sense of honor, if, in defiance of our plighted and solemn obligations, we had endured, nay, if we had not done our best to prevent, yes, and to avenge these intolerable outrages? For my part I say that sooner than be a silent witness — which means in effect a willing accomplice — of this tragic triumph of force over law and of brutality over freedom, I would see this country of ours blotted out of the pages of history. (Prolonged cheers.)

NOW THE WAR HAS COME

Winston Churchill

THIS is the same great European war that would have been fought in the year 1909 if Russia had not humbled herself and given way to German threats. It is the same war that Sir Edward Grey stopped last year. Now it has come upon us. If you look back across the long periods of European history to the original cause, you will, I am sure, find it in the cruel terms enforced upon France in the year 1870, and in the repeated bullyings and attempts to terrorize France which have been the characteristic of German policy ever since. The more you study this question the more you will see that the use the Germans made of their three aggressive and victorious wars against Denmark, against Austria, and against France has been such as to make them the terror and the bully of Europe, the enemy and the menace of every small State upon their borders, and a perpetual source of unrest and disquietude to their powerful neighbors. (Cheers.)

Now the war has come, and when it is over let us be careful not to make the same mistake or the same sort

---

This is an extract from a speech delivered at the London Opera House, September 11, 1914.

The Right Honorable Winston Leonard Spencer Churchill was born November 30, 1874. He became a member of Parliament in 1900. In turn he held the following offices under the British Crown — Under-Secretary of State for the Colonies, President of the Board of Trade, and Home Secretary. From 1911 to 1915 he was First Lord of the Admiralty. He is now an officer, serving in the British army.

4

Winston Spencer Churchill

of mistake as Germany made when she had France prostrate at her feet in 1870. Let us, whatever we do, fight for and work toward great and sound principles for the European system. And the first of those principles which we should keep before us is the principle of nationality — that is to say, not the conquest or subjugation of any great community or of any strong race of men, but the setting free of those races which have been subjugated and conquered; and if doubt arises about disputed areas of country we should try to settle their ultimate destination in the reconstruction of Europe which must follow from this war with a fair regard to the wishes and feelings of the people who live in them.

That is the aim which, if it is achieved, will justify the exertions of the war and will make some amends to the world for the loss and suffering, the agony of suffering, which it has wrought and entailed, and which will give to those who come after us not only the pride which we hope they will feel in remembering the martial achievements of the present age of Britain, but which will give them also a better and fairer world to live in and a Europe free from the causes of hatred and unrest which have poisoned the comity of nations and ruptured the peace of Christendom.

I use these words because this is a war in which we are all together, all classes, all races, all States, principalities, dominions, and powers throughout the British Empire — we are all together. Years ago the elder Pitt urged upon his countrymen the compulsive invocation, "Be one people." It has taken us till now to obey his appeal, but now we are together, and while we remain one people there are no forces in the world strong enough to beat us down or break us up. (Cheers.)

I hope, even in this dark hour of strife and struggle,

that the unity which has been established in our country under the pressure of war will not cease when the great military effort upon which we are engaged and the great moral causes which we are pursuing have been achieved. I hope, and I do not think my hope is a vain one, that the forces which have come together in our islands and throughout our empire may continue to work together, not only in a military struggle, but to try to make our country more quickly a happier and more prosperous land, where social justice and free institutions are more firmly established than they have been in the past. If that is so we shall not have fought in vain at home as well as abroad.

With these hopes and in this belief I would urge you, laying aside all hindrance, thrusting away all private aims, to devote yourselves unswervingly and unflinchingly to the vigorous and successful prosecution of the war. (Loud cheers.)

BELGIUM'S PLEA TO THE PRESIDENT

HENRY CARTON DE WIART

EXCELLENCY: His Majesty the King of the Belgians has charged us with a special mission to the President of the United States.

Let me say to you how much we feel ourselves honored to have been called upon to express the sentiments of our King and of our whole nation to the illustrious statesman whom the American people have called to the highest dignity of the Commonwealth.

As far as I am concerned, I have already been able, during a previous trip, to appreciate fully the noble virtues of the American Nation, and I am happy to take this opportunity to express all the admiration with which they inspire me.

Ever since her independence was first established, Belgium has been declared neutral in perpetuity. This neutrality guaranteed by the powers has recently been violated by one of them. Had we consented to abandon our neutrality for the benefit of one of the belligerents, we would have betrayed our obligations toward the others. And it was the sense of our international obligations as well as that of our dignity and honor that has driven us to resistance.

M. Henry Carton de Wiart, as head of the Belgian "Commission" to the United States, on September 16, 1914, addressed an appeal to the President and the people of the United States against German inhumanities to the Belgians. M. de Wiart was at the time Belgian Minister of Justice. President Wilson's reply follows.

The consequences suffered by the Belgian Nation were not confined purely to the harm occasioned by the forced march of an invading army. This army not only seized a great portion of our territory, but it committed incredible acts of violence, the nature of which is contrary to the law of nations. Peaceful inhabitants were massacred, defenseless women and children were outraged, open and undefended towns were destroyed, historical and religious monuments were reduced to dust, and the famous library of the University of Louvain was given to the flames.

Our Government has appointed a judicial commission to make an official investigation, so as to examine thoroughly and impartially the facts and to determine the responsibility thereof, and I will have the honor, Excellency, to hand over to you the proceedings of the inquiry.

In this frightful holocaust which is sweeping all over Europe, the United States has adopted a neutral attitude. And it is for this reason that your country, standing apart from either one of the belligerents, is in the best position to judge, without bias or partiality, the conditions under which the war is being waged.

It is at the request, even at the initiative, of the United States that all civilized nations have formulated and adopted at The Hague a law regulating the laws and usage of war.

We refuse to believe that war has abolished the family of civilized powers, or the regulations to which they have freely consented.

The American people has always displayed its respect for justice, its search for progress, and an instinctive attachment for the laws of humanity. Therefore, it has won a moral influence which is recognized by the entire world. It is for this reason that Belgium, bound as she is to you by ties of commerce and increasing friendship, turns to the American people at this time to let you know the real truth of the present situation. Resolved to continue unflinching defense of its sovereignty and independence, it deems it a duty to bring to the attention of the civilized world the innumerable grave breaches of rights of mankind of which she has been a victim.

At the very moment we were leaving Belgium, the King recalled to us his trip to the United States and the vivid and strong impression your powerful and virile civilization left upon his mind.

Our faith in your fairness, our confidence in your justice, in your spirit of generosity and sympathy — all these have dictated our present mission.

THE PRESIDENT'S REPLY

PERMIT me to say with what sincere pleasure I receive you as representatives of the King of the Belgians, a people for whom the people of the United States feel so strong a friendship and admiration, a King for whom they entertain so sincere a respect, and express my hope that we may have many opportunities of earning and deserving their regard.

You are not mistaken in believing that the people of this country love justice, seek the true paths of progress, and have a passionate regard for the rights of humanity.

It is a matter of profound pride to me that I am permitted for a time to represent such a people and to be their spokesman, and I am proud that your King should have turned to me in time of distress as to one who would wish on behalf of the people he represents to consider the claims to the impartial sympathy of mankind of a nation which deems itself wronged.

I thank you for the document you have put in my hands containing the result of an investigation made by a judicial committee appointed by the Belgian Government to look into the matter of which you have come

Addressed to the Royal Belgian Commission in the White House, September 16, 1914.

Woodrow Wilson was born of Scotch-Irish parents at Staunton, Virginia, December 28, 1856. His early education was obtained in private schools, and he holds degrees from a number of large universities. After practicing law for a short time, he became a teacher, and he was made president of Princeton University in 1902. From Governor of New Jersey, to which position he was elected in 1908, he became President of the United States in 1912. He was reëlected in 1916.

to speak. It shall have my utmost attentive perusal and my most thoughtful consideration.

You will, I am sure, not expect me to say more. Presently, I pray God very soon, this war will be over. The day of accounting will then come, when, I take it for granted, the nations of Europe will assemble to determine a settlement. Where wrongs have been committed their consequences and the relative responsibility involved will be assessed.

The nations of the world have, fortunately, by agreement made a plan for such a reckoning and settlement. What such a plan cannot compass, the opinion of mankind, the final arbiter in such matters, will supply. It would be unwise, it would be premature, for a single Government, however fortunately separated from the present struggle, it would be inconsistent with the neutral position of any nation, which, like this, has no part in the contest, to form or express a final judgment.

I need not assure you that this conclusion, in which I instinctively feel that you will yourselves concur, is spoken frankly because in warm friendship, and as the best means of perfect understanding between us, an understanding based upon mutual respect, admiration, and cordiality.

You are most welcome, and we are greatly honored that you should have chosen us as the friends before whom you could lay any matter of vital consequence to yourselves, in the confidence that your cause would be understood and met in the same spirit in which it was conceived and intended.

THE PLAIN DICTATES OF OUR DUTY

Herbert Henry Asquith

Four weeks ago, speaking at the Guildhall, in the City of London, when the war was still in its early days, I asked my fellow countrymen with what countenance, with what conscience, had we basely chosen to stand aloof, we could have watched from day to day the terrible unrolling of events — public faith shamelessly broken, the freedom of a small people trodden in the dust, the wanton invasion of Belgium and then of France by hordes who leave behind them at every stage of their progress a dismal trail of savagery, of devastation, and of desecration worthy of the blackest annals in the history of barbarism. That was four weeks ago. The war has now lasted for sixty days, and every one of those days has added to the picture its share of somber and repulsive traits. We now see clearly written down in letters of carnage and spoliation the real aims and methods of this long-prepared and well-organized scheme against the liberties of Europe. (Cheers.)

I say nothing of other countries. I pass no judgment upon them. But if we here in Great Britain had abstained and remained neutral, forsworn our word, deserted our friends, faltered and compromised with the plain dictates of our duty — nay, if we had not shown ourselves ready to strike with all our forces at the common enemy of civilization and freedom, there would have been nothing left for our country but to veil her face in shame and to be

In the fall of 1914 Mr. Asquith made a tour of the British Isles "summoning the nation to war." This is an extract of his speech at Cardiff on October 2, 1914.

HERBERT HENRY ASQUITH

ready in her turn — for her time would have come — to share the doom which she would have richly deserved, and after centuries of glorious life to go down to her grave, unwept, unhonored, and unsung. (Loud cheers.)

Let us gladly acknowledge what becomes clearer and clearer every day, that the world is just as ready as it ever was and no part of it readier than the British Empire, to understand and to respond to moral issues. The new school of German thought has been teaching for a generation past that in affairs of nations there is no code of ethics. According to their doctrine force and nothing but force is the test and the measure of right. As the events which are going on before our eyes have made it plain, they have succeeded only too well in indoctrinating with their creed — I will not say the people of Germany; like Burke, I will not attempt to draw up an indictment against a nation — I will not say the people of Germany, but those who control and execute German policy. (Cheers.)

But it is one of those products of German genius which, whether or not it was intended exclusively for home consumption, has not, I am happy to say, found a market abroad, and certainly not within the boundaries of the British Empire. We still believe here, old-fashioned people as we are, in the sanctity of treaties, that the weak have rights and that the strong have duties, that small nationalities have every bit as good a title as large ones to life and independence, and that freedom for its own sake is as well worth fighting for to-day as it ever was in the past. And we look forward at the end of this war to a Europe in which these great and simple and venerable truths will be recognized and safeguarded forever against the recrudescence of the era of blood and iron. (Cheers.)

THE SOLDIER OF 1914

RENÉ DOUMIC

Extract One

THE soldier of 1914. We think only of him. We live only for him, just as we live only through him. I have not chosen this subject; it has forced itself upon me. My only regret is that I come here in academician's costume, with its useless sword, to speak to you about those whose uniforms are torn by bullets, whose rifles are black with powder.

And I am ashamed, above all, of placing so feeble a voice at the service of so great a cause. But what do words matter, when the most brilliant of them would pale before acts of which each day makes us the witnesses? For these acts we have only words, but let us hope that these, coming from the heart, may bring to those who are fighting for their country somewhere near the frontier the spirit of our gratitude and the fervor of our admiration.

Our history is nothing but the history of French valor, so ingenious in adopting new forms and adapting itself each time to the changing conditions of warfare. Sol-

Rene Doumic, celebrated critic and Member of the French Academy, delivered this wonderful address to the Academy on October 26, 1914. According to the report of the Paris *Figaro*, "every sentence, every word of it was punctuated with acclamations from the audience."

We have taken two cuttings from this famous address. The other will be found under the same caption, but marked Extract Two. The speech will be found in its entirety in Volume I of the *Current History Magazine*.

diers of the King or of the republic, old "grognards" of Napoleon, who always growled yet followed just the same, youngsters who bit their cartridges with childish lips, veterans of fights in Africa, *cuirassiers* of Reichshofen, *gardes-mobiles* of the Loire, all, at the moment of duty and sacrifice, did everything that France expected of her sons.

So, too, for this war, the soldier needed has arisen. After so many heroics he has invented a new form of heroism.

I say the soldier, for the soldier is what one must say. Here begins what is clearly expressed in one phrase only — the French miracle. This national union in which all opinions have become fused is merely a reflection of the unity which has been suddenly created in our army.

When war broke out it found military France ready and armed; mere troopers, officers none of whom ever thought that he would one day lead his men under fire, and that admirable General Staff which, never allowing itself to be deflected from its purpose, did its work silent and aloof.

But there was beside this France another France, the France of civilians, accustomed by long years of peace to disbelieve in war; which, in conjuring up a picture of Europe delivered over to fire and blood, could not conceive that any human being in the world would assume the responsibility for such an act before history. War surprised the employee at his desk, the workman in his workshop, the peasant in his field. It snatched them from the intimacy of their hearths, from the amenities of family life which in France is sweeter than elsewhere. These men were obliged to leave behind beings whom they loved tenderly. For the last time they clasped in their arms the beloved partners of their lives, so deeply moved yet so

proud, and their children, the eldest of whom have understood and will never forget. And all of them, artist and
artisan, priest and teacher, those who dreamed of revenge
and those who dreamed of the fraternity of nations, those
of every age, as they stepped into their places, were en-
dowed with the soul of the soldier of France, every one
of them, and became thus the same soldier.

The war which lay in wait for these men, many of
whom did not seem made for war, was a war of which
nobody had ever seen the like. We have heard tell of
wars of giants, of battles of nations, but nobody had ever
seen a war extending from the Marne to the Vistula, nor
battles with a front of hundreds of kilometers, lasting
weeks without respite day or night, fought by millions of
men. Never in its worst nightmares had hallucinated
imagination conjured up the progress made in the art of
mowing down human lives. The German Army, to
which the German Nation has never refused anything,
either moral support or money, the nerve of war, has
been able to profit by all this progress, to reduce to a
formula the violence which drives forward the attack,
to prepare the spy system which watches over the unarmed foe, to organize even incendiarism, and to become
thus, forged by forty-four years of hatred, the most formidable tool of destruction that has ever sown ruin and
death.

The Germans arrived, with the irresistible impetus of
their masses, with the fury of a tempest, with the roar
of thunder, enraged at having been confronted on their
road by that little Belgian Nation which has just inscribed
its name among the first on the roster of heroism. Already
the German chiefs imagined themselves lords of Paris,
which they threatened to reduce to ashes — and which
did not tremble.

It was to meet this colossus of war that our little soldier marched forth. And he made it fall back.

To this new war he brings his old qualities of all time. Courage — let us not speak of that. Can one speak of courage? Just read the short sentences in the army orders.

Corporal Voituret of the Second Dragoons, mortally wounded on a reconnaissance, cries: "Vive la France! I die for her! I die happy!" Private Chabannes of the Eighteenth Chasseurs, unhorsed and wounded, replies to the Major who asks him why he had not surrendered: "We Frenchmen never surrender!" And remember those who, mortally wounded, stick to their posts so as to fight to the end with their men, and those wounded men who have but one desire — every one of us can vouch for this — to return to the firing line! And that one who, hopelessly mutilated, said to me: "It is not being crippled that hurts me; it is that I shall not be able to see the best part of the thing!" These, and the others, the thousands of others, shall we speak of their courage? — what would it mean to speak of their courage?

And the dash of them! — the only criticism to which they lay themselves open is that they are too fiery, that they do not wait the right moment for the charge, in order to drive back the enemy at the point of the bayonet. What spirit! What gayety! All the letters from our soldiers are overflowing with cheerfulness. Where, for instance, does that nickname come from applied by them to the enemy — the "Boches"? It comes from where so many more have come; its author is nobody and everybody; it is the spontaneous product of that Gallic humor which jokes at danger, takes liberties with it.

What pride! What sense of honor! Whereas the

German officer, posted behind his men, drives them forward like a flock of sheep, revolver in his hand and insults on his lips, we, on our side, hear nothing but those beautiful, those radiant words: "Forward! For your country!" — the call of the French officer to his children, whom he impels forward by giving them the example, by plunging under fire first, before all of them, at their head.

And — supreme adornment of all — with what grace they deck their gallantry! A few seconds before being killed by an exploding shell, Colonel Doury, ordered to resist to the last gasp, replies: "All right! We will resist. And now, boys, here is the password: Smile!" It is like a flower thrown on the scientific brutality of modern war, that memory of the days when men went to war with lace on their sleeves. There we recognize the French soldier such as we have always known him through fifteen centuries of the history of France.

THE SOLDIER OF 1914

RENÉ DOUMIC

Extract Two

LET us say it in a word : Never have great things been done so simply.

The soldier of 1914 knows why he is fighting. It is not for the ambition of a sovereign nor the impatience of his heir, not for the arrogance of a caste of country squires nor for the profit of a firm of merchants. No; he fights for the land where he was born and where his dead sleep; he fights to free his invaded country and give her back her lost provinces, for her past, struck to the heart by the shells that bombarded the Cathedral of Rheims; he fights so that his children may have the right to think, speak, and feel in French, so that there may still be in the world a French race, which the world needs. For this war of destruction is aimed at the destruction of our race, and our race has been moved to its depths. It has risen as one man strong and united; it has called up from its remotest history all its energy, in order to reincarnate them in the person of him whose duty is to defend the race to-day; it has inspired in him the valor of the knights of old, the endurance of the laborer bending over his furrow, the modesty of the old masters who made of our cathedrals masterpieces of anonymity, the honesty of the bourgeois, the patience of humble folk, the consciousness of duty which mothers teach to their children, all those virtues which, developed from one generation to

another, become a tradition, the tradition of an industrious
people, made strong by a long past and made to endure.
It is these qualities, all of them together, which we ad-
mire in the soldier of 1914, the complete and superb type
of the entire race.

When it has such an aim, the noblest of all, war is
sublime; all who go into it are as if transfigured. It
exalts, expands, and purifies souls. On approaching the
battlefield a holy intoxication, a holy happiness, takes
possession of those for whom has been reserved the supreme joy of braving death for their country. Death is
everywhere, but they do not believe in it any more.
And when, on certain mornings, to the sound of cannon
that mix their rumblings with mystic voices of bells, in
the devastated church which cries to the heavens through
every breach opened in its walls, the Chaplain blesses the
regiment that he will accompany the next minute to the
firing line, every head will be bent at the same time and
all will feel on their brows the breath of God.

Alas! the beauty of the struggle does not hide from
me its sadness. How many went away, full of youth and
hope, to return no more. How many have fallen already
without seeing realized what they so ardently desired;
sowers they, who to make the land fertile have watered
it with their blood, yet will not see the harvest.

But at least their sacrifice will not have been in
vain. They have brought unity to their divided country, they have made her become conscious of herself
again, they have made her learn enthusiasm once again.
They have not seen victory, but they have merited it.
Honor to them, struck down first, and glory to those who
will avenge them! We enfold them both in our devotion to the same sacred cause.

Would that a new era might dawn, thanks to them,

that a new world might be born in which we might breathe more freely, where injustices centuries old might be made good, where France, arising from long humiliation, might resume her rank and destiny!   Then, in that France, healed and revived, what an awakening, what a renewal, what a sap, what a magnificent flowering there would be!   This will be thy work, soldier of 1914!   To you we shall owe this resurrection of our beloved country.   And later on, and always, in everything beautiful and good that may be done among us, in the creations of our poets and the discoveries of our savants, in the thousand forms of national activity, in the strength of our young men and the grace of our young women, in all that will be the France of to-morrow, there will be, soldier so brave and so simple in your greatness, a little of your heroic soul!

CERTAINTY OF VICTORY

René Raphael Viviani

FAITHFUL to the signature which she attached to the treaty of September 4, 1914, and by which she engaged her honor, that is to say, her life, France, in accord with her allies, will not lay down her arms until she has avenged outraged right and regained forever the provinces which were torn from her by force, restored heroic Belgium to the fullness of her material prosperity and political independence, and broken Prussian militarism so that the Allies may eventually reconstruct a regenerated Europe founded upon justice and right.

We are not inspired, gentlemen, in this plan of war and of peace by any presumptuous hope, for we have the certainty of success. We owe this certitude to our army of all ranks and to our sailors, who, joined to the British Navy, secure for us the control of the seas, and to the

---

On December 22, 1914, René Viviani, then Premier of France, delivered in the Chamber of Deputies an address of world-wide interest, a part of which is printed below. In this speech Viviani served notice on Germany and Austria that France was in the conflict until it became possible for France and her allies to dictate terms of peace.

Viviani became Premier of France immediately after the outbreak of the war, but was succeeded by Aristide Briand in 1915. He has been called "Europe's foremost orator."

Contrast these lofty sentiments with those expressed by the German editor Maximilian Harden, in the *New Yorker Revue* (1915).

"We are waging war for ourselves alone. . . . We need land, free roads to the ocean, and for the spirit and language and wares and trade of Germany we need the same values that are accorded such goods anywhere else."

troops who have repulsed in Morocco incessant aggressions.

We owe it also to the soldiers who defend our flag in those far-off French colonies, who from the very first outbreak of the war hastened back with their tender solicitude for the mother country.

We owe it to our army, whose heroism has been guided by incomparable leaders throughout the victory of the Marne, the victory of Flanders, and in many fights, and we owe it to the nation, which has equaled this heroism by a corresponding demonstration of silence and serenity during the critical hours through which the country has passed. Thus we have shown to the world that an organized democracy can serve by its vigorous action the ideal of liberty and equality which constitute its greatness. Thus we have shown to the world, to use the words of our Commander in Chief, who is both a great soldier and a noble citizen, that "the republic may well be proud of the army that she has prepared." And thus this impious war has brought out all the virtues of our race, both those with which we were credited — of initiative, élan, bravery, and fearlessness — and those which we were not supposed to possess — endurance, patience, and stoicism.

Let us do honor to all these heroes. Glory to those who have fallen before the victory, and to those also who through victory will avenge them to-morrow! A nation which can arouse such enthusiasm can never perish.

BELGIUM SHALL RISE

Cardinal Mercier

My dearest brethren, I desire to utter, in your name and my own, the gratitude of those whose age, vocation, and social conditions cause them to benefit by the heroism of others, without bearing in it any active part.

If any man had rescued you from shipwreck or from fire, you would assuredly hold yourselves bound to him by a debt of everlasting thankfulness. But it is not one man, it is two hundred and fifty thousand men, who fought, who suffered, who fell for you, so that Belgium might keep her independence, her dynasty, her patriotic unity; so that after the vicissitudes of battle she might rise nobler, purer, more erect, and more glorious than before.

In your name I sent them the greeting of our fraternal sympathy and our assurance that not only do we pray for the success of their arms and for the eternal welfare of their souls, but that we also accept for their sake all the distress, whether physical or moral, that falls to our own share in the oppression that hourly besets us, and all that the future may have in store for us, in humiliation for a time, in anxiety, and in sorrow. In the day of final victory we shall be in honor; it is just that to-day we should all be in grief.

Extract from the famous pastoral letter of Cardinal Mercier, December 25, 1914. Since the first atrocities in Belgium Cardinal Mercier has stood forth, a tower of strength among his stricken fellow-countrymen, fearless, helpful, defiant, uncowed by vengeful threats, constantly giving aid by word and deed to his beloved land.

Cardinal Mercier

Oh, all too easily do I understand how natural instinct rebels against the evils that have fallen upon Belgium; the spontaneous thought of mankind is ever that virtue should have its instantaneous crown, and injustice its immediate retribution. But the ways of God are not our ways. Providence gives free way, for a time measured by divine wisdom, to human passions and the conflict of desires. God, being eternal, is patient. The last word is the word of mercy, and it belongs to those who believe in love.

Better than any other man, perhaps, do I know what our country has undergone. These four last months have seemed to me age-long. By thousands have our brave ones been mown down; wives, mothers, are weeping for those they shall never see again; hearths are desolate; dire poverty spreads; anguish increases. I have traversed the greater part of the districts most terribly devastated in my diocese; and the ruins I beheld were more dreadful than I, prepared by the saddest of forebodings, could have imagined. Churches, schools, asylums, hospitals, convents, in great numbers, are in ruins. Entire villages have all but disappeared.

In the dear city of Louvain, perpetually in my thoughts, the magnificent church of St. Peter will never recover its former splendor. The ancient college of St. Ives, the art schools, the consular and commercial schools of the University, the old markets, our rich library with its collections, its unique and unpublished manuscripts, its archives, its galleries — all this accumulation of intellectual, of historic, of artistic riches, the fruits of the labor of five centuries — all is in the dust.

Many a parish has lost its pastor. In my diocese alone I know that thirteen priests were put to death. Thousands of Belgian citizens have been deported to the prisons of Germany. Hundreds of innocent men have been shot or burned. We can neither number our dead nor complete the measure of our ruins.

And there where lives were not taken, and there where the stones of buildings were not thrown down, what anguish unrevealed! Families, hitherto living at ease, now in bitter want; all commerce at an end; all careers ruined; industry at a standstill; thousands upon thousands of workingmen without employment; workingwomen, shop girls, humble servant girls, without the means of earning their bread; and poor souls forlorn on the bed of sickness and fever, crying, "O Lord, how long, how long?" There is nothing to reply. The reply remains the secret of God.

Yes, dearest brethren, it is the secret of God. He is the master of events and the sovereign director of the human multitude. As for us, my brethren, we will adore Him in the integrity of our souls. Not yet do we see, in all its magnificence, the revelation of His wisdom, but our faith trusts Him with it all. Before His justice we are humble, and in His mercy hopeful.

God will save Belgium, my brethren, you cannot doubt it. Nay, rather, He is saving her. Across the smoke of conflagration, across the stream of blood, have you not glimpses, do you not perceive, signs of His love for us? Is there a patriot among us who does not know that Belgium has grown great? Nay, which of us would have the heart to cancel this last page in the national history? Which of us does not exult in the brightness of the glory of this shattered nation? When a mighty foreign power, confident in its own strength and defiant of the faith of treaties, dared to threaten us in our independence, then did all Belgians rise as one man.

Belgium gave her word of honor to defend her independence. She kept her word. The other Powers had agreed to protect and to respect Belgian neutrality. Germany has broken her word; England has been faithful to it. These are the facts. We should have acted unworthily had we evaded our obligation. And now we would not rescind our first resolution; we exult in it. Being called upon to write a most solemn page in the history of our country, we resolved that it should be also a sincere, also a glorious page. And as long as we are compelled to give proof of endurance, so long we shall endure.

Truce then, my brethren, to all murmurs of complaint. Not only to the Redeemer's example shall you look but also to that of the thirty thousand, perhaps forty thousand, men who have already shed their life blood for their country. In comparison with them what have you endured who are deprived of the daily comforts of your lives? Let the patriotism of our army, the heroism of our King and of our beloved Queen, serve to stimulate us and support us. Let us bemoan ourselves no more. Let us deserve the coming deliverance. Let us hasten it by our prayers. Courage, brethren. Suffering passes away; the crown of life for our souls, the crown of glory for our nation, shall not pass.

THERE MUST BE NO DELAY

David Lloyd George

THIS is an engineers' war, and it will be won or lost
owing to the efforts or shortcomings of engineers. Unless
we are able to equip our armies our predominance in men
will avail us nothing. We need men, but we need arms
more than men, and delay in producing them is full of
peril for this country. You may say that I am saying
things that ought to be kept from the enemy. I am not
a believer in giving any information which is useful to
him. You may depend on it he knows, but I do not
believe in withholding from our own public information
which they ought to possess, because unless you tell them
you cannot invite their coöperation. The nation that
cannot bear the truth is not fit for war, and may our
young men be volunteers, while the unflinching pride of
those they have left behind them in their deed of sacrifice
ought to satisfy the most apprehensive that we are not a
timid race, who cannot face unpleasant facts! The last
thing in the world John Bull wants is to be mollycoddled.
The people must be told exactly what the position is,

This warning against strikes was delivered to the British Nation at
Bangor on February 28, 1915.

The Right Honorable David Lloyd George was born in Manchester
in 1863 and was educated at Llanystymdwy Church School and by a
private tutor. He is the son of a Unitarian schoolmaster. From 1908–
1915 he was Chancellor of the Exchequer. In 1915 he became Minister
of Munitions and held this office until December, 1916, when the Asquith
Ministry was overthrown. Mr. Lloyd George then became Britain's
Prime Minister.

and then we can ask them to help. We must appeal for the coöperation of employers, workmen, and the general public; the three must act and endure together, or we delay and maybe imperil victory. We ought to requisition the aid of every man who can handle metal. It means that the needs of the community in many respects will suffer acutely vexatious, and perhaps injurious, delay; but I feel sure that the public are prepared to put up with all this discomfort, loss, and privation if thereby their country marches triumphantly out of this great struggle. We have every reason for confidence; we have none for complacency. Hope is the mainspring of efficiency; complacency is its rust.

We laugh at things in Germany that ought to terrify us. We say, "Look at the way they are making their bread — out of potatoes, ha, ha!" Aye, that potato-bread spirit is something which is more to dread than to mock at. I fear that more than I do even von Hindenburg's strategy, efficient as it may be. That is the spirit in which a country should meet a great emergency, and instead of mocking at it we ought to emulate it. I believe we are just as imbued with the spirit as Germany is, but we want it evoked. The average Briton is too shy to be a hero until he is asked. The British temper is one of never wasting heroism on needless display, but there is plenty of it for the need. There is nothing Britishers would not give up for the honor of their country or for the cause of freedom. Indulgences, comforts, even the necessities of life they would willingly surrender. Why, there are two millions of them at this hour who have willingly tendered their lives for their country. What more could they do? If the absorption of all our engineering resources is demanded, no British citizen will grudge his share of inconvenience.

But what about those more immediately concerned in that kind of work? Here I am approaching something which is very difficult to talk about — I mean the employers and workmen. I must speak out quite plainly; nothing else is of the slightest use. For one reason or another we are not getting all the assistance we have the right to expect from our workers. Disputes, industrial disputes, are inevitable; and when you have a good deal of stress and strain, men's nerves are not at their best. I think I can say I always preserve my temper in these days — I hope my wife won't give me away — and I have no doubt that the spirit of unrest creeps into the relations between employer and workmen. Some differences of opinion are quite inevitable, but we cannot afford them now; and, above all, we cannot resort to the usual method of settling them.

I suppose I have settled more labor disputes than any other man in this hall, and, although those who only know me slightly may be surprised to hear me say it, the thing that you need most is patience. If I were to give a motto to a man who is going to a conference between employers and workmen I would say: "Take your time; don't hurry. It will come around with patience and tact and temper." But you know we cannot afford those leisurely methods now. Time is victory, and while employers and workmen on the Clyde have been spending time in disputing over a fraction, and when a week-end, ten days, and a fortnight of work which is absolutely necessary for the defense of the country has been set aside, I say here solemnly that it is intolerable that the life of Britain should be imperiled for the matter of a farthing an hour.

Who is to blame? That is not the question, but — How is it to be stopped? Employers will say, "Are we always to give way?" Workmen say, "Employers are making their fortunes out of an emergency of the country; why are not we to have a share of the plunder?" ("Hear, hear!" and laughter.) There is one gentleman here who holds that view. (Laughter.) I hope he is not an engineer. (Renewed laughter.) "We work harder than ever," say the workmen. All I can say is, if they do they are entitled to their share. But that is not the point — Who is right? Who is wrong? They are both right and they are both wrong. The whole point is that these questions ought to be settled without throwing away the chances of humanity in its greatest struggle. There is a good deal to be said against compulsory arbitration, but during the war the Government ought to have power to settle all these differences, and the work should go on. The workman ought to get more. Very well, let the Government find it out and give it to him. If he ought not, then he ought not to throw up his tools. The country cannot afford it. It is disaster, and I believe that the moment this comes home to workmen and employers they will comply with the urgent demand of the Government. There must be no delay.

ALLIES' CONDITIONS OF PEACE

SIR EDWARD GREY

WHAT is the issue for which we are fighting? In due time the terms of peace will be put forward by our Allies in concert with us — in accordance with the alliance that exists between us — and published to the world. One essential condition must be the restoration to Belgium of her independence, national life, and free possession of her territory, and reparation to her as far as reparation is possible for the cruel wrong done to her. That is part of the great issue for which we, with our Allies, are contending, and the great part of the issue is this — we wish the nations of Europe to be free to live their independent lives, working out their own form of government for themselves, and their own national developments, whether they be great nations or small States, in full liberty. This is our ideal. The German ideal — we have had it poured out by German professors and publicists since the war began — is that of the Germans as a superior people, to whom all things are lawful in the securing of their own

On the 22d day of March, 1915, Sir Edward Grey gave to the world the conditions upon which the Allied governments would accept peace. Below is an extract from that address.

The Right Honorable Sir Edward Grey was Britain's Secretary of State for Foreign Affairs from 1905 to 1917, when he was superseded by the Right Honorable Arthur James Balfour. Grey was born April 25, 1862, and received his education at Balliol College, Oxford. Many nicknames have been given him, the best known of which is "England's Evil Genius."

power, against whom resistance of any sort is unlawful —
a people establishing a domination over the nations of
the Continent, imposing a peace which is not to be liberty
for every nation, but subservience to Germany. I would
leave the Continent altogether or even perish rather than
live on it under such conditions.

After this war we and the other nations of Europe must
be free to live, not menaced continually by talk of "supreme war lords," and "shining armor," and the sword
continually "rattled in the scabbard," and heaven continually invoked as the accomplice of Germany, free to
live without having our policy dictated and our national
destinies and activities controlled by the military caste of
Prussia. We claim for ourselves and our allies claim for
themselves, and together we will secure for Europe, the
right of independent sovereignty for the different nations,
the right to pursue a national existence, not in the shadow
of Prussian hegemony and supremacy, but in the light of
equal liberty.

All honor for ever be given from us whom age and circumstances have kept at home to those who have volun-
tarily come forward to hazard every risk, to give their
lives in battle on land and on sea. They have their
reward in enduring fame and honor. And all honor be
from us to the brave armies and navies of our Allies,
who have exhibited such splendid courage and noble
patriotism. The admiration they have aroused, and their
comradeship in arms, will be an ennobling and enduring
memory between us, cementing friendships and per-
petuating national good will. For all of us who are serving the State at home, in whatever capacity, whether
officials, or employers, or wage earners, doing our utmost
to carry on the national life in this time of stress, there is
the knowledge that there can be no nobler opportunity

than that of serving one's country when its existence is at stake, and when the cause is just and right; and never was there a time in our national history when the crisis was so great and so imperative, or the cause more just and right.

AMERICA FOR HUMANITY

Woodrow Wilson

Mr. Mayor, Mr. Secretary, Admiral Fletcher, and Gentlemen of the Fleet: This is not an occasion upon which it seems to me that it would be wise for me to make many remarks, but I would deprive myself of a great gratification if I did not express my pleasure in being here, my gratitude for the splendid reception which has been accorded me as the representative of the nation, and my profound interest in the navy of the United States. That is an interest with which I was apparently born, for it began when I was a youngster and has ripened with my knowledge of the affairs and policies of the United States.

I think it is a natural, instinctive judgment of the people of the United States that they express their power appropriately in an efficient navy, and this is true partly, I believe, because that navy somehow is expected to express their character, not within our own borders, where that character is understood, but outside our borders, where it is hoped we may occasionally touch others with some slight vision of what America stands for.

I like to image in my thought this ideal. These quiet ships lying in the river have no suggestion of bluster about them — no intimation of aggression. They are commanded by men thoughtful of the duty of citizens as well

President Wilson addressed the Mayor's Committee in New York, May 17, 1915, on the occasion of the Naval Review and Parade on the Hudson.

as the duty of officers — men acquainted with the traditions of the great service to which they belong — men who know by touch with the people of the United States what sort of purposes they ought to entertain and what sort of discretion they ought to exercise, in order to use those engines of force as engines to promote the interests of humanity.

The mission of America is the only thing that a sailor or soldier should think about: he has nothing to do with the formulation of her policy; he is to support her policy, whatever it is — but he is to support her policy in the spirit of herself, and the strength of our policy is that we, who for the time being administer the affairs of this nation, do not originate her spirit; we attempt to embody it; we attempt to realize it in action; we are dominated by it, we do not dictate it.

And so with every man in arms who serves the nation — he stands and waits to do the thing which the nation desires. America sometimes seems perhaps to forget her programs, or, rather, I would say that sometimes those who represent her seem to forget her programs, but the people never forget them. It is as startling as it is touching to see how whenever you touch a principle you touch the hearts of the people of the United States. They listen to your debates of policy, they determine which party they will prefer to power, they choose and prefer as ordinary men; but their real affection, their real force, their real irresistible momentum, is for the ideas, which men embody.

And so this sight in the river touches me merely as a symbol of that, and it quickens the pulse of every man who realizes these things to have anything to do with them. When a crisis occurs in this country, gentlemen, it is as if you put your hand on the pulse of a dynamo, it is as if the things which you were in connection with were spiritually bred. You had nothing to do with them except, if you listen truly, to speak the things that you hear. These things now brood over the river, this spirit now moves with the men who represent the nation in the navy, these things will move upon the waters in the maneuvers; no threat lifted against any man, against any nation, against any interest, but just a great, solemn evidence that the force of America is the force of moral principle, that there is not anything else that she loves and that there is not anything else for which she will contend.

ADDRESS TO THE FIGHTERS OF FRANCE

ANATOLE FRANCE

ONE hundred and twenty-six years ago to-day the people of Paris, armed with pikes and guns, to the beating of drums and the ringing of the tocsin, pressed in a long line down the Faubourg Saint-Antoine, attacked the Bastile, and, after five hours' conflict beneath deadly fire, took possession of the hated fortress. A symbolical victory won over tyranny and despotism, a victory by which the French people inaugurated a new régime.

The sovereignty of law! Therein lies the significance of the Bastile taken by the people and razed to its foundations. The coming of justice! For that reason patriots wearing the tricolor cockade in their hats, and citizenesses in frocks striped with the nation's colors, danced all night long to the accompaniment of violins, in the gay brilliance of the illuminations, on the leveled site of the Bastile.

Hour of confidence in human goodness, of faith in a future of concord and of peace! Then did France reveal her true place among men; then did she show with what hopes the Revolution swelled the hearts of Europe. The fall of the Bastile resounded throughout the whole world.

This is an extract from an article which first appeared in the *Petit Parisien*, celebrating the festival of the 14th of July, 1915. It has been translated by Winifred Stevens, editor of "The Book of France."

This Man of Letters, Jacques Anatole Thibault France, was born in Paris, April 16, 1844. Besides being an author of international repute and a member of the French Academy, Monsieur France is an officer in the Legion of Honor.

Anatole France

To Russia the good tidings came like the bright flame of a bonfire on some day of public rejoicing. In the proud city of Peter and of Catherine nobles and serfs, with tears and cries of gladness, embraced one another on the public squares. The French Ambassador at the Court of the Empress bears witness to this rapture. "It is impossible," he writes, "to describe the enthusiasm excited among tradesmen, merchants, citizens, and the young men of the upper classes by this fall of a State prison, and this first triumph of tempestuous liberty — French, Russians, Danes, Germans, Dutchmen were all congratulating and embracing one another in the streets as if they had been liberated from some onerous bondage."

In England workingmen, the middle classes, and the generous minded among the aristocracy all rejoiced over the victory of right won by the people of Paris. Neither did their enthusiasm flag, despite all the efforts of a Government strenuously hostile to the new principles of France. In 1790, the anniversary of the taking of the Bastile was celebrated in London by an immense banquet, presided over by Lord Stanhope, one of the wisest statesmen of the United Kingdom.

These are the memories we recall and the events we celebrate to-day.

Dear soldiers, dear fellow-citizens, I address you on this grave festival because I love you and honor you and think of you unceasingly.

I am entitled to speak to you heart to heart because I have a right to speak for France, being one of those who have ever sought, in freedom of judgment and uprightness of conscience, the best means of making their country strong. I am entitled to speak to you because, not having desired war, but being compelled to suffer it, I, like you, like all Frenchmen, am resolved to wage it till the end, until justice shall have conquered iniquity, civilization barbarism, and until the nations are delivered from the monstrous menace of an oppressive militarism. I have a right to speak to you because I am one of the few who have never deceived you, and who have never believed that you needed lies for the maintenance of your courage; one of the few who, rejecting as unworthy of you deceptive fictions and misleading silence, have told you the truth.

I told you in December last year: "This war will be cruel and long." I tell you now: "You have done much, but all is not over. The end of your labors approaches, but is not yet. You are fighting against an enemy fortified by long preparation and immense material. Your foe is unscrupulous. He has learned from his leaders that inhumanity is the soldier's first virtue. Arming himself in a manner undreamed of hitherto by the most formidable of conquerors, he causes rivers of blood to flow and breathes forth vapors charged with torpor and with death. Endure, persevere, dare. Remain what you are, and none shall prevail against you.

You are fighting for your native land, that laughing, fertile land, the most beautiful in the world; for your fields and your meadows. For the august mother, who, crowned with vine leaves and with ears of corn, waits to welcome you and to feed you with all the inexhaustible treasures of her breast. You are fighting for your village belfry, your roofs of slate or tile, with wreaths of smoke curling up into the serene sky. For your fathers' graves, your children's cradles.

You are fighting for our august cities, on the banks of whose rivers rise the monuments of generations — romanesque churches, cathedrals, minsters, abbeys, palaces, triumphal arches, columns of bronze, theaters, museums, town halls, hospitals, statues of sages and of heroes — monuments whose walls, whether modest or magnificent, shelter alike commerce, industry, science, and the arts, all that constitutes the beauty of life.

You are fighting for our moral heritage, our manners, our uses, our laws, our customs, our beliefs, our traditions. For the works of our sculptors, our architects, our painters, our engravers, our goldsmiths, our enamelers, our glass cutters, our weavers. For the songs of our musicians. For our mother tongue which, with ineffable sweetness, for eight centuries has flowed from the lips of our poets, our orators, our historians, our philosophers. For the knowledge of man and of nature. For that encyclopedic learning which attained among us the high-water mark of precision and lucidity. You are fighting for the genius of France, which enlightened the world and gave freedom to the nations. By this noble spirit bastiles are overthrown. And, lastly, you are fighting for the homes of Belgians, English, Russians, Italians, Serbians, not for France merely, but for Europe, ceaselessly disturbed and furiously threatened by Germany's devouring ambition.

The Fatherland! Liberty! Beloved children of France, these are the sacred treasures committed to your keeping; for their sakes you endure; for their sakes you will conquer.

EVIVA L' ITALIA

WILLIAM ARCHER

ONE of the most beautiful and memorable of human experiences is to start, some fine morning, from a point in German Switzerland or Tyrol and, in two or three days — or it may be in one swinging stretch — to tramp over an Alpine pass and down into the Promised Land below. It is of no use to rush it in a motor; you might as well hop over by aëroplane. In order to savor the experience to the full, you must take staff and scrip, like the Ritter Tannhäuser, and go the pilgrim's way. It is a joy even to pass from the guttural and explosive place names of Teutonia to the liquid music of the southern vocables — from Brieg to Domo d' Ossola, from Göschenen to Bellinzona, from St. Moritz to Chiavenna, from Botzen and Brixen to Ala and Verona. It is a still greater joy to exchange the harsh, staring colors of the north for the soft luminosity of the south, as you zigzag down from the bare snows to the pines, from the pines to the chestnuts, from the chestnuts to the trellised vineyards. And just about where the vineyards begin, you come upon two

---

William Archer, journalist and editor, was born in Perth, Scotland, on the 23d day of September, 1856. He received his education at Edinburgh University. He is widely known as a dramatic critic and has served on several of the leading European journals.

Mr. Archer's article, which appears below, was first published in the *London Daily News*, July, 1915.

wayside posts, one of them inscribed "Schweiz" or "Oesterreich," the other bearing the magic word "Italia." If your heart does not leap at the sight of it you may as well about-turn and get you home again; for you have no sense of history, no love of art, no hunger for divine, inexhaustible beauty. For all these things are implicit in the one word, "Italy."

Alas! the charm of this excursion has from of old made irresistible appeal to the northern barbarian. That has been Italy's historic misfortune. For certain centuries, under the dominance of Rome, she kept the Goths and Huns and Vandals aloof by what is called in India a "forward policy" — by throwing the outworks of civilization far beyond the Alpine barrier. But Rome fell to decay, and, wave upon wave, the barbarian — generally the Teuton, under one alias or another — surged over her glorious highlands, her bounteous lowlands, and her marvelous cities. It is barely half a century since the hated Tedeschi were expelled from the greater part of their Cisalpine possessions; and now, in the fullness of time, Italy has resolved to redeem the last of her ravished provinces and to make her boundaries practically conterminous with Italian speech and race.

The political and military aspects of the situation have been fully dealt with elsewhere; but a lifelong lover of Italy may perhaps be permitted to state his personal view of her action. While the negotiations lasted, her position was scarcely a dignified one. It seemed to be a question not, indeed, of selling her birthright for a mess of pottage, but of buying her birthright at the cost of complicity in monstrous crime. Neither Italy nor Europe would have profited in the long run by the substitution of "Belgia Irredenta" for "Italia Irredenta." But now that she has repudiated the sops offered to her honor and

conscience, her position is clear and fine. She has rejected concessions larger, probably, than any great power
has ever before been prepared to make without stroke of
sword; and she has thrown in her lot with the Allies in no
time-serving spirit, but at a point when their fortunes
were by no means at their highest. This is a gesture
entirely worthy of a great and high-spirited people.

It is true that she had no guarantee for the promised
concessions except the "Teutonica fides," which has become a byword and a reproach. But I am much mistaken
if that was the sole or main motive that determined her
resort to arms. She took a larger view. She felt that
even if Germany, by miracle, kept her faith, the world,
after a German victory, would be no place for free men to
live in. She was not moved by the care for a few square
miles of territory, more or less, but by a strong sense of
democratic solidarity and of human dignity. After the
events of the past ten months, she felt that, to a self-
respecting man or nation, German hate was infinitely
preferable to German love. It was, in fact, a patent of
nobility.

And now that Italy is ranked with us against the powers
of evil, it becomes more than ever our duty to strain every
nerve for their defeat. We are now taking our share in
the guardianship of the world's great treasure house of
historic memories and of the creations of genius. We
have become, as it were, co-trustees of an incomparable,
irreplaceable heritage of beauty. Italy has been the
scene of many and terrible wars; but since she emerged
from the Dark Ages I do not know that war has greatly
damaged the glory of her cities. She has not, of recent
centuries, had to mourn a Louvain or a Rheims. But
if the Teuton, in his present temper, should gain any
considerable footing within her bounds, the Dark Ages

would be upon her once more. What effort can be too great to avert such a calamity!

I am not by way of being versed in the secrets of Courts; but I recall to-day, with encouragement, a conversation I had some years ago with an ex-Ambassador to Italy (not a British Ambassador) who had been on intimate terms with the King, and spoke with enthusiasm of his Majesty's character. He told me of his bravery, his devotion to duty, his simple manners, his high intelligence. One little anecdote I may repeat without indiscretion. A Minister of Education said to my friend that when he had an interview with the King he felt like a schoolboy bringing up to an exacting though kindly master a half-prepared lesson; and when this was repeated to his Majesty, he smiled and said: "Ministers come and go, but I, you see, am always here." He merited far better than his grandfather (said my informant) the title of "il Re Galantuomo." Under such a Chief of State Italy may, with high hope and courage, set about her task of tearing away her unredeemed fringes from that patchwork of tyrannies known as the Austrian Empire.

RUSSIA'S HEART

MICHAEL RODZIANKO

To-DAY ends the first year of a most sanguinary war, replete with arduous sacrifices. The bloody conflict of the nations has not yet ceased and nobody can yet know when it will cease. This war is unprecedented in difficulties and sacrifices, but the greater the danger the greater grows our determination to carry it to the only possible conclusion — our decisive victory over the foe. For the solution of this problem there is now demanded from the entire country the utmost exertion of strength and complete unity.

In these days of unrest and danger our great Emperor, meeting this entire national need halfway, and wishing to listen to the voice of the Russian land, has commanded the Imperial Duma to be convened, with firm faith in the inexhaustible strength of Russia. His Majesty expects from Government and public institutions, from Russian industry, and from all the loyal sons of our native land, without distinction of views and position, united, harmonious labor for the needs of our valiant army. On this sole all-national problem, as written in the Imperial Rescript, must hereafter be concentrated all the thought of a Russia united and invincible in its unity. In the complete and clear understanding of the profound meaning of this great imperial summons, the Imperial Duma embarks upon its responsible labors.

At the time that this address was delivered, Michael Rodzianko was President of the Imperial Duma. M. Rodzianko is still President of this body, having retained his high office after the Revolution in March, 1917, because of the universal trust in his ability. On the date of the opening of the Duma, August 1, 1915, he delivered this address.

The war through which we are passing is no longer a duel of armies, but imperatively calls for the participation therein of all our people. And in their common endeavor and harmonious, united labor lies the pledge of the success of our troops over the insolent foe. Holy Russia has lived all this year with a single desire — the desire for a living and indissoluble tie with the army, and from this desire the army has drawn fiery inspiration. Our public efforts for the past year, intense but restricted within certain bounds, were favored with notable appreciation from the summit of the throne, and if these labors have actually lightened our army's difficult task of conflict with a cruel antagonist, then it must be said here with pride and a feeling of profound satisfaction that for this difficult and responsible time the public forces of Russia have inscribed a splendid page in the history of their national existence. But these efforts and labors, inspired with love for native land, are still far from sufficient.

The needs of the war are constantly growing, and from the summit of the throne has resounded afresh the summons to increased labors and new sacrifices. Our duty, sparing neither strength nor time nor means, is to set to work without delay. Let each one give his labor into the treasury of popular might. Let those who are rich, let those who are able, contribute to the welfare of the whole country. Both the army and the navy are setting us all an example of dauntless fulfillment of duty; they have accomplished all that was in human power; our turn has now arrived and the now united public strength, working ceaselessly, I am sure can supply the army with all that is necessary for its further martial exploits. For the success of these responsible public labors, in addition to the benevolent attitude of individuals placed at the head of departments, a change in the spirit itself and in the administration of the existing system is necessary. I firmly believe, gentlemen of the Imperial Duma, that at the present arduous time the reconstituted Government will not hesitate to place at the basis of its activity a trustful and responsive attitude toward the demands of public forces, summoning them thereby to common harmonious labor for the glory and happiness of Russia.

Gentlemen of the Imperial Duma! Such are the great tasks which have risen up before us in their full stature. Do not forget that upon the issue of our labors for the assistance of the army depends the greatness of independent, free, and resuscitated Russia, while in the event of their failure, both grief and humiliation may threaten her. But no, our great Mother Russia will never be the slave of anybody! Russia will fight till the last, till the complete downfall of the contemptible foe. The foe will be defeated, and until then there cannot be peace. Gentlemen, national representatives, at this great and terrible hour of trial we here must display the mighty national spirit in all its greatness. The country is awaiting a reply from you. Away with unnecessary doubts! We must fight to the end and to the last soldier capable of bearing arms. We must be strong in profound faith in the mighty Russian warrior.

We trust in thee, Holy Russia, in thy inexhaustible spiritual resources; and let this encouraging voice of the entire Russian soil penetrate thither into the glorious Russian army and into the midst of the gallant fleet, and let our glorious defenders, the army and navy, know that united Russia, burning with a single wish and a single thought, will oppose to the hostile attack the steel breasts of her sons.

THE WAR AND THE JEWS

Israel Zangwill

"You are the only people," said Agrippa, trying to hold back the Jews of Palestine from rising against the Roman Empire, "who think it a disgrace to be servants of those to whom all the world hath submitted." To-day, servants of all who have harbored them, the Jews are spending themselves passionately in the service of all. At the outbreak of the war an excited Englishwoman, hearing that the *Cologne Gazette*, said to be run by Jews, was abusing England, wrote to me, foaming at the quill, demanding that the Jews stop the paper. That the Jews as a nation do not exist, or that an English Jew could not interfere with the patriotic journalism of a German subject, nay, that the abuse in the *Cologne Gazette* was actually a proof of Jewish loyalty, did not occur to the worthy lady. Yet the briefest examination of the facts would have shown her that the Jews merely reflect their environment, if with a stronger tinge of color due to their more vivid temperament, their gratitude and attachment to their havens and fatherlands, and their

Israel Zangwill was born in London in 1864. He may be termed self-educated, for he received only a superficial and entirely elementary education in the schools of London. He became famous as the author of "Merely Mary Ann," "Ghetto Tragedies," and "The Melting Pot." He is President of the International Jewish Territorial Organization and Vice President of the Men's League for Woman Suffrage.

Zangwill's "War and the Jews" appeared in the *Metropolitan* for August, 1915. It is here reprinted by permission of the *Metropolitan Magazine*.

anxiety to prove themselves more patriotic than the patriots. It is but rarely that a Jew makes the faintest criticism of his country in war-fever, and when he does so, he is disavowed by his community and its press. For the Jew his country can do no wrong. Wherever we turn, therefore, we find the Jew prominently patriotic. In England the late Lord Rothschild presided over the Red Cross Fund, and the Lord Chief Justice is understood to have saved the financial situation not only for England, but for all her allies. In Germany, Herr Ballin, the Jew who refused the baptismal path to preferment, the creator of the mercantile marine, and now the organizer of the national food supply, stands as the Kaiser's friend, interpreter, and henchman, while Maximilian Harden brazenly voices the gospel of Prussianism, and Ernst Lissauer — a Jew converted to the religion of Love — sings "The Song of Hate." In France, Dreyfus — a more Christian Jew, albeit unbaptized — has charge of a battery to the north of Paris, while General Heymann, Grand Officer of the Legion of Honor, commands an army corps. In Turkey, the racially Jewish Enver Bey is the ruling spirit, having defeated the Jewish Djavid Bey, who was for alliance with France, while Italy, on the contrary, has joined the Allies, through the influence of Baron Sonnino, the son of a Jew. The military hospitals of Turkey are all under the direction of the Austrian Jew, Hecker. In Hungary it is the Jews who, with the Magyars, are the brains of the nation. Belgium has sent several thousand Jews to the colors and at a moment when Belgium's fate hangs upon England, has intrusted her interests at the Court of St. James's to a Jewish Minister, Mr. Hymans. Twenty thousand Jews are fighting for the British Empire, fifty thousand for the German, a hundred and seventy thousand for the Austro-Hungarian, and three hundred and fifty thousand for the Russian. Two thousand five hundred Jews fight for Serbia. Even from Morocco and Tripoli come Jewish troops — they number 20 per cent of the Zouaves. Nor are the British Colonies behind the French. From Australia, New Zealand, from Canada, South Africa, from every possession and dependency, stream Jewish soldiers or sailors. Even the little contingent from Rhodesia had Jews, and the first British soldier to fall in German Southwest Africa was Ben Rabinson, a famous athlete.

When Joseph Chamberlain offered the Zionists a plateau in East Africa the half-dozen local Britons held a "mass-meeting" of protest. Yet to-day, though the offer was rejected by the Zionists, fifty Jewish volunteers — among them Captain Blumenthal of the Artillery and Lieutenant Eckstein of the Mounted Rifles — are serving in the Defense Force enlisted at Nairobi. Letters from British Jews published in a single number of the *Jewish World*, taken at random, reveal the writers as with the Australian fighting force in Egypt, with the Japanese at the taking of Tsing-Tao, with the Grand Fleet in the North Sea, while the killed and wounded in the same issue range over almost every British regiment, from the historic Black Watch, Grenadier Guards, or King's Own Scotch Borderers down to the latest Middlesex and Manchester creations. The Old World and the New are indeed at clash when a Jewish sailor on Passover eve, in lieu of sitting pillowed at the immemorial ritual meal, is at his big gun, "my eye fixed to the telescopic lights and an ear in very close proximity to an adjacent navyphone, and the remainder of the time with my head on a projectile for a pillow." Anglo-Jewry, once the home of timorous mothers and Philistine fathers, has become a

Maccabean stronghold. One distinguished family alone — the Spielmanns — boast thirty-five members with the forces. A letter of thanks from the King has published the fact that an obscure Jew in a London suburb has five sons at the front.

And in all these armies the old Maccabean valor which had not feared to challenge the Roman Empire at its mightiest, and to subdue which a favorite General had to be detached from the less formidable Britain, has been proved afresh. "The Jewish bravery astonished us all," said the Vice Governor of Kovno, and, indeed, the heroism of the Russian Jew has become a household word. More than 300 privates — they cannot be officers — have been accorded the Order of St. George. One Jew, who brought down a German aëroplane, was awarded all four degrees of the order at once. In England Lieutenant de Pass won the Victoria Cross for carrying a wounded man out of heavy fire, and perished a few hours later in trying to capture a German sap. In Austria up to the end of the year the Jews had won 651 medals, crosses, etc. "I give my life for the victory of France and the peace of the world," wrote a young immigrant Jew who died on the battlefield. A collection of letters from German soldiers, published by the Jewish Book-shop of Berlin, reveals equal devotion to Germany. And to the question, "What shall it profit the Jew to fight for the whole world?" a Yiddish journalist, Morris Meyer, has found a noble answer. There is a unity behind all this seeming self-contradiction, he points out. "All these Jews are dying for the same thing — for the honor of the Jewish name."

AMERICA'S PART

Sir Gilbert Parker

WHAT has been the part played by the United States in this year of war? From the British standpoint, has she helped or retarded us?

The account which we render of ourselves brings no blush to our cheeks, though we differ and criticize and gibe and challenge each other, as Britishers have always done; as Americans did in the time of their Civil War, when Lincoln's heart was almost broken by opposition from his political foes, and by savage criticism of his friends. At this time we are all in a state not perfectly normal.

We are living, as it were, at the top of our being, and we are inclined to exaggerate, to be extravagant in denunciation or in criticism when things do not go as we think they ought to do, but go as they always do in war, with staggering ups and downs.

There are those among us who have thought that the United States, as a vast democracy inspired by high national ideals, and as the enemy of all reactionary and tyrannical elements, might have done more to help us in our fight for civilization, might indeed have entered the war with us.

Sir Gilbert Parker is a Canadian by birth, who has achieved fame as a novelist and man of letters. He has been most active in the spread of British and allied propaganda in the United States. This is an extract from an article which appeared in the *New York Times* on the first anniversary of the declaration of war. It is called "A Reply" and is aimed at the critics of England's policy during the first year of the great war.

But let me say — and in this I believe I speak for the great majority of British people — that we have not had the least desire to invoke the armed assistance of the United States, or to influence her in the slightest in this matter.

The United States has performed immense service to the Allies by resisting all attempts to wean or force her from her neutrality by prohibiting the export of munitions of war. Her perfect propriety and adherence to the spirit of true neutrality have resisted German pressure.

Secondly, the services she has performed to civilization by organizing relief for Belgium have been a service to humanity, and therefore a service to the Allies, who are fighting to restore to Belgium her usurped dominion.

Thirdly, the United States has rendered immense services to this country by caring for the interests of British subjects abroad, and above all, by making the lot of British prisoners of war easier. Some of the worst cruelties and inhuman oppressions have been removed by her intervention.

Lastly, her sympathy, expressed in a thousand ways, and not the least by fair consideration of the action taken by Great Britain in the blockade and other matters, has eased the minds of millions of King George's subjects. Lack of sympathy might easily have misinterpreted the acts of our Government.

I wish Americans would believe that in this country there has been since this war began a larger and truer understanding of the American people. For my own part I have known the United States intimately for many years, and I have always had faith in her national purposes and confidence in her diplomatic integrity, and, from reading her history, a realization of her sense of justice.

And in this war of ideals, fundamentally different, I believe the people of both Britain and America have come to a sense of kinship and of mutual admiration, not diminished by the possible mistakes which may have been made by Great Britain largely due to improvised organization, or in the United States by her rigid neutrality, which may not have seemed to chime with her sympathy.

American diplomacy has been unimpeachable, and we in Great Britain are grateful for an understanding which is as material a support as an army in the field.

PLEA FOR PEACE

Pope Benedict

To-day, on the sad anniversary of the terrible conflict, our heart gives forth the wish that the war will soon end. We raise again our voice to utter a fatherly cry for peace. May this cry, dominating the frightful noise of arms, reach the warring peoples and their chiefs and induce kindly and more serene intentions.

In the name of the Lord God, in the name of the Father and Lord in heaven, in the name of the blessed blood of Jesus — the price of the redemption of humanity — we implore the belligerent nations, before Divine Providence, henceforth to end the horrible carnage which for a year has been dishonoring Europe.

This is the blood of brothers that is being shed on land and sea. The most beautiful regions of Europe — this garden of the world — are sown with bodies and ruins. There, where recently fields and factories thrived, cannon now roar in a frightful manner, in a frenzy of demolition, sparing neither cities nor villages, and spreading the ravages of death.

You who before God and men are charged with the grave responsibility of peace and war, listen to our prayer, listen to the fatherly voice of the vicar of the eternal and supreme Judge to whom you should give account of your public works as well as private actions.

The abundant riches which the creating God has given

Pope Benedict XV sent out this appeal from the Vatican on the first anniversary of the great war.

Pope Benedict XV

to your lands permit you to continue the contest. But at what a price! At the price of thousands of [young lives lost each day on the battlefields, and of the ruins of so many cities and villages, so many monuments, erected through the piety and genius of our forefathers.

The bitter tears which flow in the sanctity of homes and at the foot of altars, do they not also repeat that the price of the continuation of the contest is great, too great?

And it cannot be said that the immense conflict cannot be ended without violence of arms. May this craze for destruction be abandoned; nations do not perish. Humiliated and oppressed, they tremblingly carry the yoke imposed on them and prepare their revenge, transmitting from generation to generation a sorrowful heritage of hate and vengeance.

Why not now weigh with serene conscience the rights and just aspiration of the peoples? Why not start with good will a direct or indirect exchange of views with the object of considering as far as possible these rights and aspirations, and thus put to an end the terrible combat, as has been the case previously under similar circumstances?

Blessed be he who first extends the olive branch and tenders his hand to the enemy in offering his reasonable condition of peace.

The equilibrium of world progress and the security and tranquillity of nations repose on mutual well-being and respect of the right and dignity of others more than on the number of armies and a formidable zone of fortresses.

It is the cry of peace which issues from our supreme soul this sad day and which invites the true friends of peace in the world to extend their hands to hasten the end of a war which for a year has transformed Europe into an enormous battlefield.

Let us hope for the reconciliation of the States; may the people once again become brothers and return to their peaceful labor in arts, learning, and industry; may once again the empire of justice be established; may the people decide henceforth to confine the solution of their differences no longer to the sword, but to courts of justice and equity, where the questions may be studied with necessary calm and thought.

This will be the most beautiful and glorious victory.

A STRUGGLE BETWEEN TWO WORLDS

TAKE JONESCU

IN all our long history there has never been a time of
greater gravity, or one richer in possibilities, or one more
overwhelming for us by its very grandeur, than the time
through which the world is now passing; and naturally
it affects us too, affects us more closely indeed than it
affects others.

Shall we inquire, gentlemen, what is the meaning of
that which is happening around us? Is this merely a
war like all other wars? Is it just one of those number-
less historical incidents which at first sight seem to be
important, but, as one realizes later, were of no more
than passing interest? Or are we indeed face to face
with one of those great upheavals which, occurring but
rarely, make the end of one world and the beginning of
another?

Contemporaries, gentlemen, seldom realize the importance of the events amid which they live. In their wars
they count the thousands of the slain, the millions of
money lost; but rarely do they take into account the
far-off consequences of these events, obliged as they are

This speech was delivered in the Roumanian Chamber of Deputies
during the sitting of the 16th and 17th of December, 1915.

Monsieur Jonescu has been the "strong man of Roumania" for
some time, and at all times since the outbreak of the war has championed
the cause of the Allied Powers. He it was who was chiefly responsible
for the entrance of Roumania into the war on the side of France and
England.

by the necessities of life to go on living their everyday
existence amidst the tragedy all around.

During the barbaric invasions nobody took into account what transformations they involved. Nobody
knew that therefrom might result the death of civilization for a thousand years. If people had realized the
meaning of these things, they would have made better
defense against them. At the time of the French Revolution people had no idea of the tremendous consequences
it was to bring, of the far distance they would reach.
To-day, gentlemen, I think we are confronted, not with
an ordinary war which will simply involve a certain
changing of frontiers, leaving other matters very much
as they were before. We are faced by a catastrophe
involving the whole of the human race; we have before
our eyes the declining twilight of one world, preceding
the dawn of another and a new world.

And note, gentlemen, how grave is the problem with
which humanity is faced to-day! You see Italy, instead
of accepting a gratuitous increase of territory, throwing
herself of her own free will into the horrors of war. And
it is not alone the peoples of Europe who are throbbing
with excitement to-day. Have you never asked yourselves what these new nations are doing in the great
conflict — the young Republics founded by the Anglo-
Saxons across the ocean? Why is it that we see Canada,
Australia, New Zealand enrolling from seven to eight
per cent of their populations as volunteers? Is it
for love of the mother country? Sentiment does not
move humanity to such a degree as that. How is it the
conscience of the United States of America has become
uneasy? Out of love for England? Nothing of the
sort, gentlemen. To attack Great Britain has always
been recognized as a safe and popular note by orators

in the United States. It is known as "twisting the British lion's tail." Why, then, is it disturbed, this democracy of a hundred million souls, engaged in making the most glorious experiment imaginable : the creation of a civilization without prejudices, with no class distinctions, with no monarchy, no militarism, no hindrance of any sort — a civilization based solely on nationalist sovereignty carried to its extremest limits?

This entire movement can have but one explanation, namely, that we are confronted with a transformation of the human race, a transformation which expresses itself in the form of a general massacre. It is a struggle between two worlds, and we shall see which of the two will succeed in obtaining the mastery. Were it otherwise, this war would not be possible, and it would not be waged with the fury that distinguishes it from all other wars.

Gentlemen, the truth is that in this war, which was most certainly provoked by the Germans, we see the last attempt made by a single people to secure for itself a universal hegemony.

If the German soldier were to win to-day, the first result would be that the same military force, which is the greatest in the world, would also be the greatest naval force, and there would be no more independence, no more liberty for any one in the world, not even for the great American democracy. On the day when one and the same State had domination not only on land, but also on sea — the day when the Roman Empire should be reconstituted in conformity with the affirmation once made by the Emperor William, that the hour would come when all men would be happy to call themselves German, just as formerly each exclaimed joyously *Civis romanus sum* — then the free life of each one of us would be at an end.

IT CAN BE DONE

David Lloyd George

HUNDREDS of thousands of precious lives depend upon whether you are going to bring this war to an end in a year victoriously, or whether it is going to linger on in blood-stained paths for years. Labor has got the answer. It can be done.

But I wonder whether it will not be too late. Ah, fatal words! Too late in moving here, too late in arriving there, too late in coming to this decision, too late in starting with enterprises, too late in preparing. In this war the footsteps of the allied forces have been dogged by the mocking specter of "Too late," and unless we quicken our movements damnation will fall on the sacred cause for which so much gallant blood has flowed.

I beg employers and workmen at any rate, not to have "Too late" inscribed upon the portals of their workshops, and that is my appeal. Everything depends upon it during the next few months in this war. We have had the coöperation of our allies. Great results have been arrived at. At the last conference we had of the Allies in Paris decisions were reached which will affect the whole conduct of the war. The carrying of them out depends upon the workmen of this country. The super-

---

On December 20, 1915, David Lloyd George, then Minister of Munitions in the British Cabinet, delivered this splendid criticism of the Asquith Ministry before the House of Commons. This speech, with its ever recurrent theme "too late," sounded the keynote for the downfall of the coalition cabinet.

ficial facts of the war are for the moment against us. All the fundamental facts are in our favor. That means we have every reason for looking the facts steadily in the face. There is nothing but encouragement in them if we look beneath the surface.

The chances of victory are still with us. We have thrown away many chances. But for the most part the best still remains. In this war the elements that make for success in a short war were with our enemies, and all the advantages that make for victory in a long war were ours — and they still are. Better preparation before the war, interior lines, unity of command — those belonged to the enemy. More than that, undoubtedly he has shown greater readiness to learn the lessons of the war and to adapt himself to them. He had a better conception at first of what war really meant. Heavy guns, machine guns, trench warfare — it was his study. Our study was for the sea. We have accomplished our task to the last letter of the promise. But the advantages of a protracted war are ours. We have an overwhelming superiority in the raw material of war. It is still with us in spite of the fact that the Central Powers have increased their reserves of men and material by their successes.

The overwhelming superiority is still with us. We have the command of the sea that gives us ready access to neutral countries, and, above all — and this tells in a long war — we have the better cause. It is better for the heart — nations do not endure to the end for a bad cause. All these advantages are ours. But this is the moment of intense preparation. It is the moment of putting the whole of our energies at home into preparing for the blow to be struck abroad. Our fleet and the gallantry of the troops of our allies have given us time to muster our reserves. Let us utilize that time without the loss of a moment. Let us cast aside the fond illusion that you can win victory by an elaborate pretense that you are doing so. Let us fling to one side rivalries, trade jealousies, jealousies professional or political. Let us be one people — one in aim, one in action, one in resolution, so to win the most sacred cause ever intrusted to a great nation.

BELGIUM'S DEBT TO FRANCE

Henry Carton de Wiart

During the dark hours through which we are now passing, Belgium, fettered and mute, treats with stoic disdain both the brutality and the insinuating attitude alternating in the system of oppression imposed upon her by the enemy. Worn by suffering, he would like her to call for Peace in a wail of woe that would be heard even at Havre! He flatters himself that he can compel her to betray her companions in this struggle. By misdirected advice in the press, he endeavors to influence the members of the Belgian Government. Their slightest acts, and even their silence, being misconstrued, commented upon, and distorted into signs and tokens of a desire for making a separate peace, by which means Germany hopes to break up the insurmountable resistance of her adversaries. Gentlemen, the Belgian people have resolved to suffer till the hour of deliverance; justice and inevitable reparation have sounded for her, she follows the example of her Great Cardinal, that pure image of ardent patriotism!

Belgium, in the darkness that surrounds her, in the silence of imprisonment which separates her from the rest of the world, has heard with a thrill the distant booming of the cannon at Verdun. She understands a great

---

A great French-Belgian demonstration was held in Paris, March 11, 1916, at the Sorbonne. M. de Wiart, Belgian Minister of Justice, rendered homage, in these words, to France and Frenchmen.

struggle is going on there at present, in which French valor forms a rampart for the liberty of nations against the insane power that has sworn to enslave them. The future of Europe depends upon the annihilation of Prussian militarism; more especially the future of small nations, desirous of living and flourishing in freedom, in order to contribute by their labor and efforts towards the general progress of humanity. History has taught us that the equilibrium of European power is never disturbed but momentarily under the thrust of conquerors, and that it can always counteract the oscillations their ambition would like to create therein.

So it will be now. Violence and brutal strength cannot kill the lives of peoples having the will to live. The map of Europe may be modified, but it will not be traced in one and the same shade of color, indicating a sort of Holy Germanic Empire, a parody and resurrection of the past. The elements of those races having given proof of their vitality, will finally reconstitute themselves and renew their existence in common, flourishing in an atmosphere which has been purified by the gentle breath of peace. The small nations will not then forget what they owe to France.

TOAST TO PREMIER ASQUITH

Signor Antonio Salandra

To the illustrious guest who by his presence in Rome at this solemn hour in the history of the world has desired to give us a living proof of the solidarity of the ties which bind the great British Empire to new Italy, I express with much pleasure and emotion the greetings of the Parliament and Government of Italy.

Parliament and Government are, in Italy as in England, bound together in an indissoluble harmony, working under the supreme guarantee of the national monarchy — a monarchy which is the protector of all the most ardent aspirations of civil and social progress. And since your noble efforts, in which, it must be remembered, we coöperated with all our power, were unsuccessful in warding off the premeditated conflict which for twenty months has been drenching the world with blood, Parliament and the Government, in Italy as in England, have repeatedly affirmed their determination not to lay down their arms until our just cause has been victorious.

Immediately after the adjournment of the historic "Conference of the Allies" in Paris on March 28, 1916, Premier Asquith of Great Britain made a visit to Rome. The visit had as its objective, of course, a "closer cementing of the friendship" between Italy and Great Britain.

Antonio Salandra was born at Troia, near Foggia, in 1853. For several years he was a professor in the University of Rome. In 1891 he was made Under Secretary of State for Finance and for the Treasury in 1893. He became Prime Minister of Italy in 1914, but was replaced by Paolo Boselli in August, 1916.

How firm and unshakable our determination is you will be told to-morrow by the grandson of Victor Emmanuel the Great, who will show you the dogged efforts which our nation in arms puts forth every day against the immense obstacles of nature and the powerful defenses of the enemy. We, who humbly but with firmness of heart are proceeding to carry out our arduous tasks, inspired by the ideals of the immortal authors of our united Italy, recall how your country always gave them generous and inspiring sympathy. We recall those associates in the glorious peace of history — Giuseppe Mazzini surrounded by affectionate veneration, Giuseppe Garibaldi hailed as a conqueror, Camillo di Cavour honored in the greatest assembly of the modern world with tributes which have never been given any other foreign statesman. We recall Gladstone denouncing those Governments which oppressed us, and Palmerston who wished to keep open the sea-routes for the ships of the Thousand.

You worthily occupy the place of your great predecessors, who will never die in the grateful memory of Italians ; towards you there will go out from our people a feeling of lively sympathy and confidence, of which, as of the warmth of our sun, I hope you will take back a kindly impression to your country. You can say to your fellow countrymen that the Parliament and Government of Italy, henceforward free, are proud to carry out the last act of our national Resurrection, bound to you by an indissoluble tie of interests, forces, and ideals. I drink to your Excellency's health, to the greatness of the British Empire in peace and freedom, and to the victory of the Allied arms.

TOAST TO ITALY AND SIGNOR SALANDRA

HERBERT HENRY ASQUITH, PRIME MINISTER OF GREAT BRITAIN

THE reception which you have given me here to-day and the kind and eloquent words of your Excellency give me peculiar gratification. As an old Parliamentarian myself, it delights me to have an opportunity of exchanging fraternal salutations with the members of the Senate and the Chamber of Deputies.

Parliamentary institutions took their rise in England, and after many centuries of experience, in all free countries, they have been found, with all their imperfections, to be the best instrument that has been devised for the interpretation and the effective action of national opinion in the domain of government.

As you, Sir, have reminded me, the friendship — may I not say the affection — between Italy and my country is not a plant of recent growth. I can, myself, remember the time when Italy was still divided by the accidents of history, and the efforts of the great patriots whose names you have recalled were directed to the double object of expelling the last remnants of foreign rule, and uniting in one body, as they had long been united in spirit, all the constituent elements of your integral national life. In every stage of that struggle it is not an exaggeration to say that the emancipators of Italy had with them the

---

This is the reply of Mr. Asquith to Signor Salandra's toast on the occasion of his (Asquith's) visit to Rome in March, 1916.

unfailing interest, the unbounded sympathy, and the inextinguishable hopes of the British people.

In truth, Sir, diverse in many ways as have been the lines of our development, the national life in our two countries is to a large extent fed from the same sources and animated by the same spirit. Hatred of tyranny, love of justice, the passion for liberty, the sense of the equality of all men before the law, free opinion, free speech — these are the ideas that are held and the principles of policy which are practiced with equal ardor and conviction in Great Britain and in Italy. No wonder, then, that the years since your unity was finally achieved have been years of unbroken friendship between the two nations — a friendship which no misunderstanding or mischance has ever been allowed even for a moment to imperil.

Such were our happy relations before the war. To-day we are not only friends but Allies, finding in our common efforts, our common sacrifices, and our common hopes a new and ever more intimate bond of union. We watch with equal pride the glorious gallantry and skill of the Allied Armies and Navies. This is not a war which can be won merely by the multiplication of fighting men and the accumulation of munitions and material. It calls for the organization, the coördination, the concentration in due proportion and proper perspective of all the various resources of the Allies. We have to work in concert, not only in the battlefield, not only on the high seas, not only in the air above and under the waters, but also in the not less essential domain of industry, of transport, of finance. Finally, I ask, could these efforts and sacrifices be inspired by a worthier cause? Independence for the smaller and weaker states, respect for treaties and for public law, resolute resistance to the supremacy of brute force; in a word — for these are all means to an end — the free life of a free Europe. Together we stand or fall; and standing together, as we do, we shall achieve a decisive and durable victory, not for ourselves alone but for posterity, for the future of civilization, for the dearest and most precious interests of humanity.

THE SIGNIFICANCE OF THE CONFLICT

Baron Rosen

Aside from all political, economic, and psychological motives, the deep significance of the conflict before us, and the source of the determination of the Allies to fight to a finish against Germany's desire to dominate by brutal force the whole world, is the conviction rooted in the public mind that the German doctrine of "Might is Right" constitutes the gravest danger to the human race, and cannot be tolerated.

In such a just cause the whole civilized world should have been on the side of the Allies, especially the countries geographically so situated that they are in danger of having to share the fate of brave and hapless Belgium. Why is it, then, that in reality their attitude is somewhat indifferent? It is undoubtedly in our power to remove one of the causes which make the public opinion in neutral countries hesitate about taking up an attitude favorable to us.

In this war against German absolutism, in this struggle for right and justice, and for the freedom and independence of the smaller nations, we fight hand-in-hand with the

This speech was delivered in June, 1916, by Baron Rosen in the Upper Chamber of the Russian Duma.

The speaker, formerly ambassador to the United States, is one of the ablest men in Russia. The particular significance of this liberal speech was that it voiced the spirit of liberal Russia nine months before the Revolution. As a result of it, Baron Rosen was dismissed from the appointive Upper Council, and the final reaction toward despotism set in, which led directly to the Revolution. The speech is, therefore, really historic.

BARON ROMANOVITCH ROSEN

most advanced peoples in Europe, and we cannot win the sympathy of the civilized world unless we bring our internal front, so to speak, on a level with the political ideas of our valiant allies, and apply them in the administration of our border provinces and in the government of the nationalities forming part of the population of Russia.

There are two diametrically opposed methods of government. One is the method adopted by our allies. Its results were seen in the enthusiastic outbursts of patriotism throughout the self-governing British Colonies, and even among the non-English elements — the Irish, French-Canadians, Boers, and Indians. They all rushed to the defense of the British Empire. Thanks to this method of government it was possible for England to intrust the chief command of the troops in South Africa to that very general who, sixteen years ago, led the Boers against the English, and who is now Prime Minister of British South Africa.

The other method is that of the Germans. They have applied it to the population of Posen, Schleswig, Alsace and Lorraine, with the result that even the pure German portion of the population of Alsace retained its passionate attachment for France, who never treated them as second-rate citizens, or as possible traitors to their country.

In our policy toward our border provinces, and toward the so-called non-Russian nationalities, we have, to the greatest detriment of the real interests of Russia, followed closely the German system of government. We have even improved upon it by an addition of medieval religious intolerance. People may say that war is decided by military power and not by the degree of sympathy which neutral countries may show for the home policy of this or that State. The German Government obviously regards the question in a different light, or else it would not be spending millions on propaganda in all countries, even the remotest in the world. Not only do we not counteract this propaganda, but by our domestic policy we supply our enemies with weapons with which to set against us the public opinion of such countries as the United States of America — the only great neutral power — and our neighbor Sweden. It is inconceivable that those who guide our home policy should not be able to realize that by our medieval treatment of the Jewish population of Russia, and by our systematic outrages upon the constitutional habit of mind of the Finnish people, we are helping enormously the pro-German propaganda in neutral countries which our enemies carry on with lavish means to the detriment of the cause of the Allies. The question is, why has not our Government settled these questions once and for all, as it did — alas, so late — the question of Polish autonomy? The only answer is that our Government did not wish to renounce a traditional policy so dear to the hearts of our militant Nationalists.

It is therefore incumbent upon the Legislative Chambers to assist the Government in this matter, and to introduce bills abolishing all the restrictive laws against the Jews, and canceling the laws of July 17 concerning Finland. Such measures would undoubtedly facilitate the task of the Government in international matters, and would meet with the lively appreciation of our valiant allies.

We must bear in mind that this great European War is not only a conflict of interests, but also of ideas and principles. In fighting against German militarism, Russia is taking her stand on the side of those who fight for the triumph of the idea of Right and Freedom, and it is necessary that in Russia there shall henceforth be no people oppressed or deprived of their inherent rights.

THE RÔLE OF FRANCE IN THIS WAR

RAYMOND POINCARÉ

AT the call of their country in danger they started up, seized their weapons, and hurried forth to protect their frontiers. Old as well as young, fathers as well as sons, shed their blood in one sublime cause — the safety of their country and the future of humanity.

The French had too frequently shown their bravery, for any one to dare to doubt their military worth; but, on the strength of I know not what legend, we were believed to be incapable of long-thought-out plans and tenacious effort. Two years have passed without shaking French resolution, without weakening French constancy.

It is because we have offered invincible resistance, not only to the blows inflicted by the German armies, but also to insidious German propaganda and campaigns for demoralization, that the Allied Staffs have been able to come to an understanding which is daily growing more definite, that their governments are more closely united and that our combined action has, with time, and under favorable impulse acquired more strength and power.

Just as our country during these long months has given splendid proof of its patience, reflexion, and sang-froid, so

---

"On July 14, 1916, France's National Fête Day, at an official ceremony organized in Paris in memory of the men who have died for their country, M. Poincaré, in the presence of battalions from all the allied troops, justly rendered homage to our departed heroes." — Taken from the Paris Chamber of Commerce Bulletin.

our generals, officers, non-commissioned officers and men
— whom France loves to associate together in her praise,
for they all share the glory of the battlefield — are entitled to have some of the finest pages in the annals of our
history consecrated to their memory.

During endless weeks, under the concentrated fire of
artillery of all calibers, over ground soaked with rain,
and ploughed up by shells, our battalions, defying the
enemy, defended the outposts of Verdun step by step,
unaware until the last few days how greatly their endurance and stoicism would facilitate the combined operations of the Allies elsewhere.   Humanity has never yet
witnessed any sight of more heroic grandeur.

The Central Empires can retain no illusion as to the
possibility of reducing the Allies and wresting from their
lassitude a peace which for the Prussian militarists would
be but a stratagem wherewith to mask preparation for
fresh aggression.   It is in vain that our enemies study the
military map which they used to invoke with such boast-
ful satisfaction.   They perceive now with uneasiness,
that, on the Somme as on the Styr, at the foot of the
Karpathians as on the summits of the Alps, the lines upon
that changing map have already been altered consider-
ably, and they know that to make it complete, it is necessary to add thereto the seas which are closed to them,
and the colonies which have been taken from them.
They well know also that the strength of the belligerent
countries is not so much reckoned on the geographical
position of field-trenches, as upon the condition of| the
fighting troops, their reserves, their capacity for attacking
and for resisting attack, and upon the moral temper of
the peoples and armies.

As for us, we shall not fail, even if we were fighting for
honor alone, and we are fighting for honor and for life.

To be, or not to be, is the poignant problem before the great European nations, and for a free democracy such as ours it would be "not to be," if we vegetated, struggling in the suffocating and unhealthy shadow of a German Empire, strong enough to hold over the whole of Europe its heavy hegemony.

No, by the grief of our French families, by the long torture of our occupied country, by the blood of our soldiers; no, we shall not suffer our sorrow to weaken our will! The more we hate war, the more passionately must we labor to prevent its return, the more must we work and pray that peace may bring us together with the complete restitution of our invaded provinces — invaded provinces of yesterday, and invaded provinces of forty-six years ago — the reparation of Right violated at the expense of France and the Allies, and the guarantees necessary to the definitive safeguarding of our national freedom.

VERDUN

Raymond Poincaré

GENTLEMEN, these walls mark the spot where the greatest hopes of imperial Germany were dashed to pieces. It
was here that she sought to achieve blustering ostentatious
success, and here that France quietly and firmly replied:
"You shall not pass." When the attack against Verdun
began, on February 21st, the enemy had a double objective in view: he intended to forestall a general offensive
on the part of the Allies; and at the same time to strike a
blow, that would be much talked of, by rapidly capturing
a fortress whose historical fame would, in the eyes of the
German people, increase its military importance. The
ruins of these Germanic dreams are now lying at our feet.

The splendid troops, who, under the command of
Generals Petain and Nivelle, held out against the formidable onslaught of the German Army for many long months,
frustrated the enemy's designs by their valor and their
spirit of self-sacrifice. It is they who have enabled all
our Allies to work, with increasing activity, for the pro-
duction of war material; it is they who have now bril-
liantly marked by the light of their heroism the boundary
of Germanic force, thus imparting to the world confidence
in our final victory; in short, it was the resistance of these

This speech was delivered at Verdun, September 13, 1916. The
occasion for the address was the conferring of medals and decorations
upon the heroic city of Verdun, "in recognition of its valorous defense,"
by the French and Allied Governments. The ceremony took place in
the casements of the citadel.

troops which, by assuring the realization of the plan formed by the different Staffs, left Russia time to carry out her triumphant offensives of June 4th and July 2d. It also enabled Italy to make her brilliant attack on Gorizia, on June 25th, and, from July 1st on, allowed the Anglo-French forces to conduct their offensive on the Somme. It also permitted the army of the East to make its preparations, to concentrate its different elements, and lend fraternal assistance to our new Allies, the Rumanians, in their conflict with Germano-Bulgarians. Honor to the soldiers of Verdun! they sowed the seed of the coming harvest and watered it with their blood.

You see here, gentlemen, the just return of things. The name of Verdun, to which Germany in her fond dream had given a symbolic signification that was to have shortly evoked — she thought — in the minds of men, a brilliant defeat for our armies, together with the irremediable discouragement of our country and the passive acceptance of a German peace; this name stands, henceforth, in neutral countries, and among our Allies, for what is noblest, purest, and best in the French character. It has become, so to speak, a synonym for Patriotism, Bravery, and Generosity. Throughout the ages, in every corner of the globe, the name of Verdun will resound like a shout of Victory and Joy, sent up by a free human race.

THE WAR'S LEGACY OF HATRED

MAURICE MAETERLINCK

BEFORE we reach the end of this war, whose days of grief and terror now seem to be numbered, let us weigh for the last time in our minds the words of hatred and malediction which it has so often wrung from us.

We have to deal with the strangest of enemies. He has deliberately, scientifically, in full possession of his senses, without necessity or excuse, revived all the crimes which we had believed to be forever buried in the barbarous past. He has trampled under foot all the precepts which the human race had so painfully gleaned out of the cruel darknesses of its origins; he has violated all the laws of justice, of humanity, of loyalty, of honor, from the highest, which almost touch the divine, to the simplest and most elementary, which still appertain to the lower orders. There is no longer any doubt on this point. The proof of it has been established and reëstablished, the certitude definitively acquired.

But, on the other hand, it is no less certain that the enemy has displayed virtues which it would not be right for us to deny; for one honors one's self by recognizing

In October of 1916 this article appeared in *Les Annales*, Paris. It was later translated for the *Current History Magazine*, through whose courtesy it is here reprinted.

The Belgian Maeterlinck, born 1862, is well known on this side of the Atlantic as an author and playwright. He began publishing his works about 1890. Among his best-known plays are "Pelleas and Melisande," "The Blue Bird," and "The Unknown Guest."

the valor of those whom one combats. He has gone to death in deep, compact, disciplined masses, with a blind, obstinate, hopeless heroism, for which history furnishes no example equally somber, and which often has compelled our admiration and our pity.

I am well aware that this heroism is not like that which we love. For us heroism should be, above all, voluntary, free from all restraint, active, ardent, joyous, spontaneous; whereas with them it is mixed with much of servility, of passivity, of sadness, of gloomy, ignorant submission, and of fears more or less base. Yet in a moment of peril these distinctions vanish for the most part; no force on earth could drive toward death a nation that did not have within itself the will to confront death.

Our soldiers have not deceived themselves on this point. Ask those who return from the trenches. They execrate the *enemy;* they have a horror of the aggressor, unjust, arrogant, gross, too often cruel and perfidious; they do not hate the *man*, they pity him; and, after the battle, in the defenseless wounded or the disarmed prisoner they recognize with astonishment a brother in misery who, like themselves, has been trying to do his duty, and who has laws which he considers high and necessary. Underneath the intolerable enemy they see the unfortunate mortal who likewise is bearing the burden of life.

Leaving out of account the unpardonable aggression, and the inexpiable violation of treaties, very little is lacking to make this war, despite its madness, a bloody but magnificent testimonial of grandeur, of heroism, of the spirit of sacrifice. Humanity was ready to raise itself above itself, to surpass all that it had achieved up to this hour. And it has done it. We have not known of nations that were capable, through months and years, of renouncing their rest, their security, their wealth, their well-being, all that they possessed and loved, even life itself, to accomplish what they believed to be their duty. We had never seen whole nations that were able to understand and admit that the happiness of each of those living at the moment of trial does not count when it is a question of the honor of those no longer living or of the happiness of those not yet born.

Here we stand on summits that had never before been attained. And if, on the part of our enemies, this unexampled renunciation had not been poisoned at its source, if the war which they wage against us had been as beautiful, as loyal, as generous, as chivalrous as that which we wage against them, one might believe that it was to be the last war, and that it was to end, not in mortal combat, but in the awakening from a bad dream with a noble and fraternal astonishment. They have not permitted this to be so; and it is their deception, we may rest assured, that the future will have the greatest difficulty in pardoning.

Now, what are we going to do? Must we go on hating to the end of our days? Hatred is the heaviest load that man can bear on this earth, and we should be bowed down by the burden. But, on the other hand, we do not wish to be again the victims of trust and love. Here once more our soldiers, in their clear-eyed simplicity and nearness to truth, anticipate the future and teach us what is best to do and not to do. As we have seen, they do not hate the individual, but they do not trust him. They do not see the human being in him until he is unarmed. They know from sad experience that as long as he has weapons he does not resist the mad impulse to injure, to betray, to kill, and that he becomes good only when he is powerless.

Is he thus by nature, or has he been made thus by those

who lead him? Have the chiefs carried away the whole nation, or has the whole nation driven its chiefs? Have the leaders made the people like themselves, or have the people chosen the leaders and supported them only because they resembled themselves? Did the disease come from below or from above, or was it everywhere? This is the great obscure point of the awful adventure. It is not easy to explain, and it is still less easy to find an excuse.

If they prove that they have been deceived and corrupted by their masters, they are proving at the same time that they are less intelligent, less firmly grounded in justice, honor, and humanity — in a word, less civilized — than those whom they pretend to have a right to subjugate in the name of a superiority which their own demonstration annihilates; on the other hand, if they do not prove that their errors, their perfidies, and their cruelties, — which can no longer be denied — are to be imputed solely to their masters, these sins fall back upon their own heads with all their pitiless weight. I do not know how they will escape the horns of this dilemma, nor what decision will be rendered by the future, which is wiser than the past, even as the morning, to quote the old Slavic proverb, is wiser than the night. Meanwhile let us imitate the prudence of our admirable soldiers, who know better than we do what path to follow.

FRANCE AND THE NEW COMMANDMENTS

Paul Deschanel

LET us hearken to the voice of the trench and the tomb; what comes from there is a cry of love. Never has the French family been more united. Frenchmen were following different roads, but they have come together at the summit. The same devotion, the same ideal! The heroes facing death know that before the brief flame of life is extinguished in them it lights another, it is immortal. And the enemy does not comprehend that the thing which was tearing us apart is what is now uniting us: the passion for right.

France of St. Louis, of Joan of Arc, of St. Vincent de Paul, of Pascal; France of Rabelais, of Descartes, of Molière, of Voltaire; France of the Crusades and France of the Revolution, you are sacred to us, and your sons are equal in our hearts as they are in the face of peril. Those who do not discover the common peak under the same rays have not looked long enough or far enough.

Yes, this sublime array of youth goes to death as to a higher life. Will that higher life be the life of France?

Paul Eugène Louis Deschanel has held several of the highest offices in the gift of the French Nation, being several times President and Vice President of the French Chamber of Deputies. He was born in 1856 and obtained his education at the College St.-Barbe. He has published many studies of social, political, and economic conditions in his native land.

The address here given was delivered on the occasion of the meeting of the Academics of the Institute of France in Paris, October 26, 1916.

The great silence of these deserts full of men, where the cannon alone speaks, will not hover above them forever. Controversy is the soul of progress. It is because it has been lacking in Germany that the world is on fire.

I do not know whether the phrase, "conflict of the classes," still expresses the meaning of those who formerly employed it, for since 1914 not a single voice in Germany has been raised against the invasion of Belgium and France; but never have men seen more clearly the grandeur of poverty, the obligations of wealth, the truth that souls are not measured by conditions. There are the things that one possesses and the things that one values, and the two comprise the whole patrimony of a nation. The little white crosses which mark our battlefields from the Marne to the Seine and from the sea to the Vosges are terrible masters of equality. May they draw the living closer together!

The invasion of Belgium, the burning of Louvain and Rheims, the assassination of Miss Cavell, the torpedoing of steamships, the murder of Jacquet, the execution of Captain Fryatt, the uprooting of the civil populations in our invaded provinces, the rallying of all the professors of law to justify these crimes — these things indicate a nation overcome by vertigo, like those hordes on the Yser which rushed forward in serried columns, drunk with ether. One imagines above their heads the Valkyries of Walhalla and the fierce divinities of their impenetrable forests. "Let insolence germinate," says Æschylus in "The Persians"; "what grows up is the fruition of crime; one gathers a harvest of sorrows."

And now we hear repeated every day: "We must destroy German militarism, the Prussian military caste." Yes, without doubt; and even in Germany the abusive privileges of that caste have called forth jeers, protests in the press, in fiction, in the theater, in the Reichstag. But we know how the Saverne affair ended. It is the army that has created independence; it is the army that guarantees the power and wealth of the empire. Germany is proud of it, loves it, has made a cult of it. Her "intellectuals," better informed on that point than the stranger who judges others by himself, cry: "We resent it that the enemies of Germany dare to oppose German science to what they call Prussian militarism. The spirit of the army is the same as that of the nation."

The truth is that in Germany, as elsewhere, national sentiment has been strongest; it has carried all before it, rivalries of caste, of class, and of creed. To judge a nation aright one must look upon the whole of it at once, like the aviator who hovers above the ocean and sees currents which others cannot see.

If Frenchmen ought to know Germany better, they ought also to make France better known. "A worn-out nation!" said Bismarck. "A degenerate people!" cried William II. Worn-out, degenerate, the France of Pasteur, of Berthelot, of Henri Poincaré! A worn-out nation, a degenerate people, the France of Renan and Taine, which for forty years, in all lines of thought, in poetry, philosophy, history, drama, fiction, criticism, has magnetized the minds of the world! A degenerate nation, the nation that has produced at the same time illustrious musicians and pleiades of painters, sculptors, architects, engravers, such as the world had not seen since the Renaissance! Worn out, the nation which, between two wars, has created the second largest colonial empire in the world! And tell me: in what country, in what epoch, have the hopes and aspirations of mankind found finer orators?

Our institutions were supposed to be unworthy to endure, and yet they resist the most enormous upheaval of all the ages. The republic was not to be allowed to conclude alliances, and yet France has never had more allies, or more powerful ones.

And mark the climax! Yes, even after Marathon, Salamis, and Platæa, even after Valmy, Jemappes, and Fleurus, France touches the highest peak; for Athenian civilization was founded on slavery, and the armies of the Revolution were restricted armies, while to-day it is all France that is fighting — for all men! Through her we are living the greatest life that men have ever lived, for what is the life of humanity if not an increase of justice?

THE DAY OF THE DEAD

Maurice Maeterlinck

OUR memories are peopled by a multitude of heroes, stricken in the flower of youth, and far different from that procession of yore, pale and worn out, which counted almost solely the aged and sickly, who were already scarcely alive when they left this earth. To-day in all our houses, in town, in country, in palace, and in cottage, a young man dead lives and rules in all the beauty of his strength. He fills the poorest, darkest dwelling with glory, such as it had never dreamed of. It is terrible that we should have this experience, the most pitiless mankind has known, but, now that the ordeal is nearly over, we can think of the perhaps unexpected fruits which we shall reap.

One will soon see the breach widening and destinies diverging between those nations which have acquired all these dead and all this glory, and those who have been deprived of them and it. And one will be astonished to find that those which have lost most are those which will have kept their wealth, and their men. There are losses which are priceless gain, and there are gains in which one's future is lost. There are dead whom the living cannot replace and whose memory does things which no living bodies can do, and we are each of us now agents of some one greater, nobler, braver, wiser, and more alive

---

This is an extract from Maeterlinck's beautiful tribute to Belgium's dead. It first appeared in the *Paris Figaro* on All Souls' Day, 1916.

MAURICE MAETERLINCK

than ourselves. He will be, with all his comrades, our judge.

If it be true that the dead weigh the souls of the living and that our fate depends upon their verdict, he will be our guide and our champion. For this is the first time since history revealed to us her catastrophes that man has felt round about him and within him the influence of such a multitude of heroic dead.

ENGLAND'S ANSWER

David Lloyd George

I APPEAR before the House of Commons to-day with the most terrible responsibility that can fall upon the shoulders of any living man. As the chief Minister of the Crown, and in the midst of the most stupendous war in which this country ever has been engaged, a war upon which its destinies depend, the responsibilities which rest upon the government have been accentuated by the declaration of the German Chancellor, and I propose to deal with that at once.

The statement made by him in the German Reichstag has been followed by a note presented to us by the United States Minister, without any note or comment. The answer which is given by the government will be given in full accord with all our various Allies. Already there has been an interchange of views, not upon the note itself, because it has only recently arrived, but upon the spirit which impelled the note. The note is only a paraphrase of the speech, so that the subject matter of the note itself has been discussed informally with the Allies, and I am

The reply of David Lloyd George to the German Chancellor's peace proposals has been called "one of the most important speeches ever made in the history of the world." It was sent through the United States Government to the Allied Powers.

Mr. George appeared before the House of Commons on the afternoon of December 19, 1916, and delivered this historic address. It was his first speech as the head of the British Government. He had accepted the Premiership only a few days before.

glad to be able to say that we arrived separately at iden-
tical conclusions.

I am very glad that the first answer was given to the
German Chancellor by France and by Russia. They have
unquestionably the right to give the first answer. The
enemy is still on their soil and their sacrifices have been
greater. The answer they have given has already appeared in all the papers, and I stand here to-day on behalf
of the government to give a clear and definite support to
the statement they have already made. And here let me
say that any man or set of men who wantonly and without sufficient cause prolongs a terrible conflict like this
has on his soul a crime that oceans could not cleanse; on
the other hand, a man or set of men, who from a sense of
war-weariness abandoned the struggle without achieving
the high purpose for which we entered upon it, would be
guilty of the costliest poltroonery ever perpetrated by
any statesman.

I should like to quote the well-known words of Abraham Lincoln under similar conditions:

"We accepted the war for an object, a worthy object.
The war will end when that object is attained. Under
God I hope it will never end until that time."

Are we to achieve that object by accepting the invita-
tions of the German Chancellor? That is the only question we have to put to ourselves.

There has been some talk about the proposals of peace.
What are those proposals? There are none. To enter
into a conference, on the invitation of Germany, proclaiming herself victorious, without any knowledge of the
proposals she intends to make, is putting our heads into
a noose with the rope end in the hands of the Germans.

This country is not altogether without experience in
these matters. This is not the first time we have fought

a great military despotism overshadowing Europe, and it won't be the first time we have helped to overthrow a military despotism.

We have an uncomfortable historical memory of these things, and can recall one of the greatest of these despots, whose favorite device was to appear in the garb of an angel of peace, either when he wished time to assimilate his conquests or to reorganize his forces for fresh conquests; or, secondly, when his subjects showed symptoms of fatigue and war-weariness, an appeal was always made in the name of humanity. He demanded an end to the bloodshed at which he professed himself horrified, although he himself was mainly responsible.

Our ancestors were taken in once, and bitterly they and Europe rue it. The time was devoted to reorganizing his forces for a deadlier attack than ever upon the liberties of Europe. Examples of this kind cause us to regard this note with a considerable measure of reminiscent disquietude.

We feel we ought to know before we give favorable consideration to such an invitation, whether Germany is prepared to accede to the only terms on which it is possible for peace to be obtained and maintained in Europe.

What are these terms? They have been repeatedly stated by all the leading statesmen of the Allies. All I can do is to quote what the leader of the House, Mr. Bonar Law, said last week when he made practically the same statement of terms as those put forward by Mr. Asquith — "restitution, reparation, guarantees against repetition." So that there shall be no mistakes (and it is important that there should be no mistake in a matter of the life and death of millions), let me say complete restitution, full reparation, and effectual guarantees.

Did the German Chancellor use a single phrase that

would indicate that he was prepared to accept such terms? Was there a hint of restitution? Was there any suggestion of reparation? Was there any indication of any security for the future, that this outrage on civilization would not again be perpetrated at the first profitable opportunity?

The very substance and style of the speech constituted a denial of peace on the only terms on which peace is possible. He is not even conscious now that Germany has committed an offense against the rights of free nations. Listen to this quotation: "Not for an instant had they (the Central Powers) swerved from the conviction that a respect for the rights of free nations is not in any degree incompatible with their own rights and legitimate interests." When did they discover that? Where was the respect for the rights of other nations in Belgium?

That, it is said, was for self-defense. Menaced, I suppose, by the overwhelming army of Belgium, the Germans were intimidated into invading Belgium, burning Belgian cities and villages, massacring thousands of inhabitants, old and young, carrying others into slavery at the very moment when the note was being written about the "unswerving conviction of the respect for the rights of other nations."

What guarantee is there that these terrors will not be repeated in the future? That if we enter into a treaty of peace, we shall put an end to Prussian militarism? If there is to be no reckoning for these atrocities by land and sea, are we to grasp the hand which perpetrated them without any reparation being made? We have to exact damages. We have begun; already it has cost us much. We must exact it now, so as not to leave such a grim inheritance for our children. Much as we all long for peace, deeply as we are horrified at the war, their note and speech give small encouragement to hope for an honorable and lasting peace. What hope is given in that speech? The whole root and cause of this bitterness — the arrogant spirit of the Prussian military caste — will it not be as dominant as ever if we patch up a peace now? The very speech resounds with the boast of the Prussian military triumph; the very appeal for peace was delivered ostentatiously from the triumphal chariot of Prussian militarism.

We must keep a steadfast eye on the purpose for which we entered the war. Otherwise the great sacrifices we are making will be all in vain. The German note states that for the defense of their existence and for the freedom of national development the Central Powers were constrained to take up arms. Such phrases cannot but deceive those who listen to them. They are intended to deceive the German nation into supporting the designs of the Prussian military caste.

Who ever wished to put an end to their national existence or to the freedom of their national development? We welcomed their development so long as it was on behalf of peace. The greater their development in that direction, the greater would humanity be enriched by that development.

That was not our design and it is not our purpose now. The Allies entered into this war to defend Europe against the aggression of Prussian military domination, and they must insist that the end is a most complete and effective guarantee against the possibility of that caste ever again disturbing the peace of Europe.

Prussia, since she got into the hands of that caste, has been a bad neighbor — arrogant, threatening, bullying, shifting boundaries at her will, taking one fair field after another from weaker neighbors and adding them to her own dominions, ostentatiously piling up weapons of offense, ready on a moment's notice to be used. She has always been an unpleasant, disturbing neighbor to us. She got thoroughly on the nerves of Europe, and there was no peace near where she dwelt. It is difficult for those who were fortunate enough to live thousands of miles away, to understand what it has meant to those who lived near. Even here, with the protection of the broad seas between us, we know what a disturbing factor the Prussians were with their constant naval menace. But even we can hardly realize what it has meant to France and Russia. Several times there were threats. There were two of them within the lifetime of this generation which presented an alternative of war or humiliation.

There were many of us who had hoped that internal influences in Germany would have been strong enough to check and ultimately to eliminate this hectoring. All our hopes proved illusory, and now that this great war has been forced by the Prussian military leaders upon France, Russia, Italy, and ourselves, it would be a cruel folly not to see to it that this swashbuckling through the streets of Europe to the disturbance of all harmless and peaceful citizens shall be dealt with now as an offense against the law of nations.

The mere word that led Belgium to her own destruction will not satisfy Europe any more. We all believed it; we all trusted in it. It gave way at the first pressure of temptation, and Europe has been plunged into this vortex of blood. We will therefore wait until we hear what terms and guarantees the German Government offers other than those, better than those, surer than those, which she so lightly broke. Meanwhile we ought to put our trust in an unbroken army rather than in a broken faith.

A LEAGUE FOR PEACE

WOODROW WILSON

THE equality of nations upon which peace must be founded if it is to last must be an equality of rights ; the guarantees exchanged must neither recognize nor imply a difference between big nations and small, between those that are powerful and those that are weak. Right must be based upon the common strength, not upon the individual strength, of the nations upon whose concert peace will depend. Equality of territory or of resources there of course cannot be ; nor any other sort of equality not gained in the ordinary peaceful and legitimate development of the peoples themselves. But no one asks or expects anything more than an equality of rights. Mankind is looking now for freedom of life, not for equipoises of power.

And there is a deeper thing involved than even equality of right among organized nations. No peace can last, or ought to last, which does not recognize and accept the principle that governments derive all their just powers from the consent of the governed, and that no right anywhere exists to hand peoples about from sovereignty to sovereignty as if they were property. I take it for granted, for instance, if I may venture upon a single

On January 22, 1917, the President of the United States delivered before the Senate a speech which his admirers claim to be the "most important pronouncement of an American president since the Monroe Doctrine."

example, that statesmen everywhere are agreed that there should be a united, independent, and autonomous Poland; and that henceforth inviolable security of life, of worship, and of industrial and social development should be guaranteed to all peoples who have lived hitherto under the power of governments devoted to a faith and purpose hostile to their own.

I speak of this, not because of any desire to exalt an abstract political principle which has always been held very dear by those who have sought to build up liberty in America, but for the same reason that I have spoken of the other conditions of peace which seem to me clearly indispensable, — because I wish frankly to uncover realities. Any peace which does not recognize and accept this principle will inevitably be upset. It will not rest upon the affections or the convictions of mankind. The ferment of spirit of whole populations will fight subtly and constantly against it, and all the world will sympathize. The world can be at peace only if its life is stable, and there can be no stability where the will is in rebellion, where there is not tranquillity of spirit and a sense of justice, of freedom, and of right.

So far as practicable, moreover, every great people now struggling towards a full development of its resources and of its powers should be assured a direct outlet to the great highways of the sea. Where this cannot be done by the cession of territory, it can no doubt be done by the neutralization of direct rights of way under the general guarantee which will assure the peace itself. With a right comity of arrangement no nation need be shut away from free access to the open paths of the world's commerce.

And the paths of the sea must alike in law and in fact be free. The freedom of the seas is the sine qua non of peace, equality, and coöperation. No doubt a some-what radical reconsideration of many of the rules of international practice hitherto thought to be established may be necessary in order to make the seas indeed free and common in practically all circumstances for the use of mankind, but the motive for such changes is convinc-ing and compelling. There can be no trust or intimacy between the peoples of the world without them. The free, constant, unthreatened intercourse of nations is an essential part of the process of peace and of develop-ment. It need not be difficult either to define or to secure the freedom of the seas if the governments of the world sincerely desire to come to an agreement concerning it.

It is a problem closely connected with the limitation of naval armaments and the coöperation of the navies of the world in keeping the seas at once free and safe. And the question of limiting naval armaments opens the wider and perhaps more difficult question of the limitation of armies, and of all programs of military preparation. Difficult and delicate as these questions are, they must be faced with the utmost candor and decided in a spirit of real accommodation, if peace is to come with healing in its wings, and come to stay. Peace cannot be had without concession and sacrifice. There can be no sense of safety and equality among the nations if great prepon-derating armaments are henceforth to continue here and there to be built up and maintained. The statesmen of the world must plan for peace, and nations must adjust and accommodate their policy to it as they have planned for war and made ready for pitiless contest and rivalry. The question of armaments, whether on land or sea, is the most immediately and intensely practical question connected with the future fortunes of nations and of mankind.

I have spoken upon these great matters without reserve and with the utmost explicitness because it has seemed to me to be necessary if the world's yearning desire for peace was anywhere to find free voice and utterance. Perhaps I am the only person in high authority amongst all the peoples of the world who is at liberty to speak and hold nothing back. I am speaking as an individual, and yet I am speaking also, of course, as the responsible head of a great Government, and I feel confident that I have said what the people of the United States would wish me to say. May I not add that I hope and believe that I am in effect speaking for liberals and friends of humanity in every nation and of every program of liberty? I would fain believe that I am speaking for the silent mass of mankind everywhere who have as yet had no place or opportunity to speak their real hearts out concerning the death and ruin which they see has come already upon the persons and the homes they hold most dear.

And in holding out the expectation that the people and Government of the United States will join the other civilizations of the world in guaranteeing the permanence of peace upon such terms as I have named, I speak with the greater boldness and confidence because it is clear to every man who can think that there is in this promise no breach in either our traditions or our policy as a nation, but a fulfilment, rather, of all that we have professed or striven for.

I am proposing, as it were, that the nations should with one accord adopt the doctrine of President Monroe as the doctrine of the world; that no nation should seek to extend its polity over any other nation or people, but that every people should be left free to determine its own polity, its own way of development, unhindered, unthreatened, unafraid, the little along with the great and powerful.

I am proposing that all nations henceforth avoid entangling alliances which would draw them into competitions of power, catch them in a net of intrigue and selfish rivalry, and disturb their own affairs with influences intruded from without. There is no entangling alliance in a concert of power. When all unite to act in the same sense and with the same purpose, all act in the common interest and are free to live their own lives under a common protection.

I am proposing government by the consent of the governed; that freedom of the seas which in international conference after conference representatives of the United States have urged with the eloquence of those who are the convinced disciples of liberty; and that moderation of armaments which makes of armies and navies a power for order merely, not an instrument of aggression or of selfish violence.

These are American principles, American policies. We could stand for no others. And they are also the principles and policies of forward looking men and women everywhere, of every modern nation, of every enlightened community. They are the principles of mankind and must prevail.

FRANCE UNITED IN THE CAUSE OF RIGHT

Paul Deschanel

AFTER thirty-one months of the most terrible of wars, France is as united as she was on the very first day of hostilities. The crime committed by Germany brought about this miracle. All Frenchmen to-day have but one thought, one ardent desire, and that is to drive out the enemy. A German peace would be but a truce for more wars in the near future. If we cease the struggle to-day, our sons will have to go on with it.

A few weeks since, a deputy from the invaded regions, on coming back to take his seat in the Chamber of Deputies after an absence of two years and a half, said: "They are suffering cruelly there, both in body and soul; they are enduring the greatest humiliations; they have insufficient food; yet, full of determination, they cry to you saying: 'Whatever you do, make no premature peace, no patched-up, no German peace.'" We who are free, and far from the struggle, shall we be less determined, less patient and enduring than they are? The noble cry of these our oppressed brothers is heard throughout France, even to her remotest hamlet; the whole country, from the Alps to the Pyrenees, from the

---

In February of 1917, a great meeting of representative French Associations was held at the Sorbonne. M. Deschanel was in the chair, supported by President Poincaré, the members of the Government and of the diplomatic corps. The chairman addressed the meeting, affirming "the indissoluble union of all Frenchmen in opposing German aggression."

Ocean to the Front, has risen up in wrath, in pride, and hope!

We are approaching the most decisive moment of all times. This war is the greatest of all wars, not only by the length of the battle-line, the power of inventions, the number of men and the peoples engaged in it — fourteen nations, twenty million men, are wrestling, amidst untold horrors — but because all the moral inheritance of mankind is at stake. It is no longer a duel between two countries, or two civilizations, Greece and Persia, Rome and Carthage; it is a struggle between the just and the unjust, between honor and perjury, between right and crime. The morality of the universe itself is at stake.

Germany had guaranteed the independence and neutrality of Belgium; she called upon this country to allow her a passage through her land in order to attack France; Belgium refused, and Germany ruthlessly fell upon her and slew her. Germany has, before God, before man, and before the ages to come, stained herself forever with the blood of innocent Belgium. If such a crime should triumph, the human race would be degraded. Treaties would no longer have any value, nations no security — you see that neutral countries are already endangered. All moral effort since the human race has existed would be annihilated, and man be on a level with the beasts; the strongest paw, the sharpest claw, would rule the world. The very thought of such a terrible state of existence is maddening. Any one who has a heart would brave the worst evils rather than sink to such degradation.

Germany would like to assume the domination of the world, but by what right? By right of her own superiority, so she says. And wherein lies this vast superiority? Is it in her methods of observation which have failed? She was mistaken in her judgment of France, Belgium, Britain, Russia, Italy, and Japan. She understands things, but not men, nor their souls, and yet she wishes to rule and lead them! The Germans say: "Our enemies want to annihilate us." These are but idle words! A nation of seventy million inhabitants cannot be annihilated; and I suppose that when people talk about "destroying Prussian militarism," they don't imagine they can change the Prussian character. Prussia is a military State and can never be anything else. If she had not been such, she would never have existed. It would be necessary, too, to overthrow the German university, school, and pulpit, for her army is only the offspring of these.

No! we are not pursuing some mere fancy or dream; we do not wish to prevent any one from living, but what we do want is that nations may breathe freely and work in peace, in independence and dignity.

AMERICA BREAKS WITH GERMANY

WOODROW WILSON

I CANNOT bring myself to believe that the Imperial German Government will indeed pay no regard to the ancient friendship between their people and our own, or to the solemn obligations which have been exchanged between them, and will destroy American ships and take the lives of American citizens in the wilful prosecution of the ruthless naval program they have announced their intention to adopt. Only actual overt acts on their part can make me believe it even now.

If this inveterate confidence on my part in the sobriety and prudent foresight of their purpose should unhappily prove unfounded; if American ships and American lives should in fact be sacrificed by their naval commanders in heedless contravention of the just and reasonable understandings of international law and the obvious dictates of humanity, I shall take the liberty of coming again before the Congress to ask that authority be given me to use

On February 3, 1917, at two o'clock, the United States, through its President, notified the world that it had broken off diplomatic relations with the Imperial German Government. As President Wilson entered the House, the whole throng rose and cheered him. "Grim faced and solemn" he was escorted to his place and began to read the document which "was heard round the world."

Not a sound came from floor or galleries but the clear, calm tones of the President, speaking slowly and distinctly. The great assemblage of legislators and notables listened with the closest attention to words which recorded "one of the somber moments of American and world history."

any means that may be necessary for the protection of our seamen and our people in the prosecution of their peaceful and legitimate errands on the high seas. I can do nothing less. I take it for granted that all neutral governments will take the same course.

We do not desire any hostile conflict with the Imperial German Government. We are the sincere friends of the German people and earnestly desire to remain at peace with the government which speaks for them. We shall not believe that they are hostile to us unless and until we are obliged to believe it; and we purpose nothing more than the reasonable defense of the undoubted rights of our people.

We wish to serve no selfish ends. We seek merely to stand true alike in thought and in action to the immemorial principles of our people which I sought to express in my address to the Senate only two weeks ago — seek merely to vindicate our right to liberty and justice and an unmolested life.

These are the bases of peace, not war. God grant that we may not be challenged to defend them by acts of wilful injustice on the part of the government of Germany.

DEMOCRACY AND THE WAR

ALBERT THOMAS

WHEN celebrating the birthday anniversary of the first president of the United States, the Government of this Republic not only performs a duty of international courtesy, but it conveys the homage of grateful France to one of her noblest citizens. Upon the threshold of the history of our two Democracies stands a warlike hero whose image is almost as familiar to French schoolboys as it is to American children; he is the stubborn fighter of Valley Forge, the victor at Yorktown: General Washington, who was appointed by Congress "to command all the Continental forces, raised, or to be raised, for the defense of American liberty."

It is the nobleness of wars inspired by a democratic ideal, which arouses beyond the seas the enthusiasm of free races. They are wars of sentiment, but they are also wars of determination and will.

When material interests or dynastic ambitions are at stake, governments wearied of a conflict may be led to compromise matters, but nations like ours never grow weary of defending their liberty.

Washington's ideal was that the long war he had waged should assure peace and prosperity to the United States

At the ceremony held in Paris on the anniversary of George Washington's birthday, February 22, 1917, M. Albert Thomas, Minister of Munitions, called to remembrance the ideals by which the sister democracies were actuated, and paid homage in eloquent terms to the memory of our first President, "upon whom, in 1793, the Legislative Assembly had bestowed the title of French Citizen."

forever, and that the Union should serve as a model and example to less privileged countries, still slaves to tradition. "It would be worthy of a free and enlightened nation, soon to become a great one, to give humanity the magnanimous and novel example of a race always guided by the high principles of justice and generosity."

We know these same motives inspire President Wilson, for in his address to the Senate he said: "America has entertained from her birth the lofty and honorable expectation of being able to point out to Humanity, by her manner of being and doing, the path that leads to Liberty."

But in order to remain true to this ideal of liberty and peace, America has gradually been compelled to abandon the isolation recommended by Washington at a time when the history of the world was little more than the history of Europe.

President Wilson now desires the Monroe Doctrine to be applied to the whole universe, saying:

"I suggest that the different nations should agree to adopt the Monroe Doctrine as the doctrine of the world; that no nation should seek to impose its policy upon any other country, but that each race should be free to determine its own particular policy, to choose its own way of development, without anything to hinder, molest, or dismay it, in such a manner that we may see the small country prospering by the side of the great and powerful one."

These ideas, though familiar to Frenchmen, seem to-day both daring and ancient. They are ancient, for in the hope of bringing back human society to a state of natural kindness and perpetual peace, we cannot fail to find again the spirit of our revolutionary ancestors! They are daring ideas, because the last half-century of European history, and these thirty months' war, have compelled us to acknowledge that the way towards that Golden Age is long and that all the nations would not tread the same path and keep step with us! But, gentlemen, what a comfort it is to our people to feel that your country is also considering the stages that have to be traveled over!

It is not by mere chance that the words which most clearly define the spirit of France at war were uttered by the most illustrious representatives of American democracy: Washington and Lincoln.

Remember the exhortation given at the consecration of Gettysburg cemetery: "Let us resolve that these men shall not have died in vain, so that the nation may, by the help of God, be restored to liberty, and that government of the people, by the people, and for the people shall not perish from the earth."

These striking words make an echo, more than two thousand years after, to the funeral oration uttered by Pericles in honor of the warriors who had died to save Athens. They bear an untold weight of meaning for France, who is determined to fight to the finish for her liberty, for they are a pledge of faith in an undying democracy.

THE PRESIDENT'S WAR MESSAGE

WOODROW WILSON

WE are now about to accept the gauge of battle with the Imperial German Government, this natural foe to liberty, and shall, if necessary, spend the whole force of the nation to check and nullify its pretensions and its power. We are glad, now that we see the facts with no veil of false pretense about them, to fight thus for the ultimate peace of the world and for the liberation of its peoples, the German peoples included; for the rights of nations great and small, and the privilege of men everywhere to choose their way of life and of obedience.

The world must be made safe for democracy. Its peace must be planted upon the trusted foundation of political liberty.

We have no selfish ends to serve. We desire no conquest, no dominion. We seek no indemnities for our-

---

In an address even "more memorable" than his speech on the occasion of the breaking off of diplomatic relations with Germany, President Wilson outlined his reason for declaring that war existed between the United States and the Imperial German Government. In the late hours of the evening of April 2, 1917, he appeared before the 65th Congress, in special session assembled, and delivered this new Declaration of Rights. The editors of our newspapers have been practically unanimous in declaring this one of the greatest of our state documents.

Mr. Gilbert K. Chesterton, in commenting on this speech, said that Mr. Wilson was "truly and worthily the orator of the human race. The simple words with which he ended are among the sort of historic sayings that can be graven on stone. 'God helping her she can do no other.' That is the answer of humanity to all possible preaching about the inhumanity of war, to the most that can be said, to the worst that can be endured."

selves, no material compensation for the sacrifices we shall freely make.

We are but one of the champions of the rights of mankind. We shall be satisfied when those rights have been made as secure as the faith and the freedom of the nations can make them.

Just because we fight without rancor and without selfish objects, seeking nothing for ourselves but what we shall wish to share as free peoples, we shall, I feel confident, conduct our operations as belligerents without passion, and ourselves observe with proud punctilio the principles of right and of fair play we profess to be fighting for.

It will be all the easier for us to conduct ourselves as belligerents in a high spirit of right and fairness because we act without animus, not in enmity towards a people or with the desire to bring any injury or disadvantage upon them, but only in armed opposition to an irresponsible government, which has thrown aside all considerations of humanity and of right and is running amuck.

We shall, happily, still have an opportunity to prove our friendship in our daily attitude and actions towards the millions of men and women of German birth and native sympathy who live amongst us and share our life, and we shall be proud to prove it towards all who are in fact loyal to their neighbors and to the government in the hour of test. They are, most of them, as true and loyal Americans as if they had never known any other fealty or allegiance. They will be prompt to stand with us in rebuking and restraining the few who may be of a different mind and purpose. If there should be disloyalty it will be dealt with with a firm hand of stern repression; but if it lifts its head at all it will lift it only here and there and without countenance except from a lawless and malignant few.

Gentlemen of the congress, it is a distressing and oppressive duty which I have performed in thus addressing you. There are, it may be, many months of fiery trial and sacrifice ahead of us. It is a fearful thing to lead this great peaceful people into war, into the most terrible and disastrous of all wars, civilization itself seeming to be in the balance.

But the right is more precious than peace, and we shall fight for the things which we have always carried nearest our hearts, — for democracy, for the right of those who submit to authority to have a voice in their own governments, for the rights and liberties of small nations, for a universal dominion of right by such a concert of free peoples as shall bring peace and safety to all nations and make the world itself at last free.

To such a task we can dedicate our lives and our fortunes, everything that we are and everything that we have, with the pride of those who know that the day has come when America is privileged to spend her blood and her might for the principles that gave her birth and happiness and the peace which she has treasured. God helping her, she can do no other.

FRANCE CONGRATULATES AMERICA

Raymond Poincaré

At the moment when, under the generous inspiration of yourself, the great American republic, faithful to its ideals and traditions, is coming forward to defend with the force of arms the cause of justice and liberty, the people of France are filled with the deepest feelings of brotherly appreciation.

Permit me again to give you, Mr. President, in this solemn and grave hour, an assurance of the same sentiments of which I recently gave you evidence, sentiments, which under the present circumstances have grown in depth and warmth.

I am confident that I voice the thought of all France in expressing to you and to the American nation the joy and pride which we feel to-day as our hearts again beat in unison with yours.

This war would not have reached its final import had not the United States been led by the enemy himself to take part in it. To every impartial spirit it will be apparent, in the future more than ever in the past, that German imperialism, which desired, prepared and declared this war, had conceived the mad dream of establishing its hegemony throughout the world. It has succeeded only in bringing about a revolt of the conscience of humanity.

This message was cabled on April 5, 1917, by President Poincaré to President Wilson.

Raymond Poincaré

In never-to-be-forgotten language you have made yourself, before the universe, the eloquent interpreter of outraged laws and a menaced civilization.

Honor to you, Mr. President, and to your noble country. I beg you to believe in my devoted friendship.

MESSAGE TO AMERICA

David Lloyd George

AMERICA has in one bound become a world power in a sense never before. America waited until she found a cause worthy of her traditions.

The American people held back until they were fully convinced the fight was not a sordid scrimmage for power and possessions, but an unselfish struggle to overthrow sinister conspiracy against human liberty and human rights.

Once that conviction was reached, the great republic of the west has leaped into the arena and stands now side by side with the European democracies, who, bruised and bleeding after three years of grim conflict, are still fighting the most savage foe that ever menaced the freedom of the world.

The glowing phrases of the President's noble deliverance will illumine the horizon and make clearer than ever the goal we are striving to reach.

There are two phrases which will stand out forever in the story of this crusade, — first, "that the world must be made safe for democracy" — next, that "the menace to peace and freedom lies in the existence of autocratic governments backed by organized force and controlled wholly by their will and not by the will of their people."

On April 6, 1917, Lloyd George, speaking for the Cabinet, and "all the people and all the nations of the British Empire," commended America on her stand in entering the world war.

These words represent the faith which inspires and sustains our people in the tremendous sacrifices they have made and are still making.

They also believe the unity of peace maintained can only rest upon democracy, upon the rights of those who submit to authority to have a voice in their government; upon the respect for the rights and liberties of nations both great and small, and upon universal dominion of the public right.

To all these the Prussian military autocracy is an implacable foe.

The Imperial war cabinet, representing all the people and all the nations of the British empire, wish me in their behalf to recognize the chivalry and courage which calls the people of the United States to dedicate the whole of their resources and service to the greatest cause that ever engaged human endeavor.

GREETINGS FROM A SISTER REPUBLIC

M. Ribot and M. Deschanel

M. Ribot

You have heard the admirable message of President Wilson. We all feel that something important, something which exceeds the proportions of a political event, has been accomplished.

It is a historic fact of unequaled import — this entry into the war on the side of us and our allies of the most peaceable democracy in the world. After having done everything to affirm its attachment to peace, the great American nation declares solemnly that it cannot remain neutral in this immense conflict between right and violence, between civilization and barbarism. It holds that honor requires it to take up the challenge flung at the rules of international law so laboriously built up by civilized nations. (Applause.)

But at the same time it declares that it is not fighting for self-interest, that it desires neither conquest nor compensation, that it intends only to help toward a victory of the cause of law and liberty. (The deputies rise and applaud.)

The grandeur, the nobility, of this action is enhanced by the simplicity and serenity of the language of the illustrious leader of that great democracy. (Applause.)

These two speeches were made on April 6, 1917, in the French Chamber of Deputies. M. Ribot was Minister of Foreign Affairs; M. Deschanel, President of the Chamber. The two speeches were widely circulated throughout France by the order of the Government.

If the world had entertained the least doubt of the profound meaning of this war in which we are engaged, the message of the President of the United States would dissipate all obscurity. It makes apparent to all that the struggle is verily a struggle between the liberal spirit of modern societies and the spirit of oppression of societies still enslaved to military despotism. It is for this reason that the message rings in the depths of all hearts like a message of deliverance to the world. (Applause.)

The people who, under the inspiration of the writings of our philosophers, declared their rights in the eighteenth century, the people who place Washington and Lincoln foremost among their heroes, the people who in the last century suffered a civil war for the abolition of slavery, were indeed worthy to give such an example to the world.

Thus do they remain faithful to the traditions of the founders of their independence, and demonstrate that the enormous rise of their industrial strength and of their economic and financial power has not weakened in them that need for an ideal without which there can be no great nation. (Applause.)

What touches us particularly is that the United States has held to the friendship which at an earlier time was ratified in blood. We bear witness with grateful joy to the enduring sympathy between the peoples, which is one of the delicate virtues the bosom of a democracy can nourish.

The Star-spangled Banner and the Tricolor will fly side by side; our hands will join; our hearts beat in unison. This will mean for us, after so much suffering, heroically borne, so many bereavements, so many ruins, a renewal of the sentiments which have animated and sustained us during this long trial. The powerful, decisive aid which the United States brings us is not only a material aid; it will be especially moral aid, a real consolation. (Applause.)

Seeing the conscience of peoples everywhere in the world awake and rise in an immense protest against the atrocities of which we are the victims, we feel more keenly that we are fighting not only for ourselves and for our allies, but for something immortal, and that we are laying the foundations of a new order. Thus our sacrifices will not have been in vain; the generous blood poured out by the sons of France will have fertilized the seeds both of justice and of liberty so fundamentally necessary to concord between nations. (Applause.)

In the name of the whole country, the government of the French Republic addresses to the government and people of the United States, with the expression of its gratitude, its warmest good wishes. (Prolonged cheers.)

M. DESCHANEL

The French Chamber greets with enthusiasm the verdict of the President of the Republic of the United States, and the vigorous decision of the Federal Senate accepting the war imposed by Germany.

Æschylus says in "The Persians": "When insolence takes root, it grows into crime; the harvest is suffering." And we can say: "The growth of the crime brings vengeance; after the harvest of suffering comes the harvest of justice!" (Applause.)

The cry of the women and children from the depths of the abyss where hideous wickedness flung them has echoed from one end of the earth to the other. Washington and Lincoln trembled in their graves; their spirit has roused America. (Applause.)

But is it a question only of avenging Americans? Is it a question of punishing only the violation of treaties signed by the United States? No; the eternal truths proclaimed in the Declaration of 1776, the sacred causes which Lafayette and Rochambeau defended, the ideals of a pure conscience from which the great Republic was born — honor, morality, liberty — these are the supreme values which shine in the folds of the Star-spangled Banner. (Applause.)

Descendants of the Puritans of New England, brought up on the precepts of the Gospel, who under the eyes of God are about to punish the infernal creation of evil, falsehood, perjury, assassination, profanation, rape, slavery, martyrdom, and disasters of every kind; Catholics struck to the heart by curses against their religion, by outrages against their cathedrals and statues, reaching a climax in the destruction of Louvain and of Rheims; university professors, trustworthy guardians of law and learning; industrialists of the East and Middle West, farmers and agriculturists of the West; workmen and artisans, threatened by the torpedoing of vessels, by the interruption of commerce, revolted by the insults to their national colors — all are arrayed against the mad arrogance which would enslave the earth, the sea, the heavens, and the souls of men. (Prolonged applause.)

At a time when, as in the heroic times of the American Revolution, the Americans are to fight with us, let us repeat once more: We wish to prevent no one from living, working, and trading freely; but the tyranny of Prussia has become a peril for the New World as for the Old, for England as for Russia, for Italy as for Austria, and for Germany itself. To free the world, by a common effort of all democratic peoples, from the yoke of a feudal and military caste in order to found peace upon right, is a work of human deliverance and universal good. (Applause.)

In accomplishing, under an administration henceforth immortal, the greatest act in its annals since the abolition of slavery, the glorious nation whose whole history is but a development of the idea of liberty remains true to its lofty origin and creates for itself another claim to the gratitude of mankind. (Applause.)

The French Republic, across the ruins of its cities and its monuments, devastated without reason or excuse by shameful savagery, sends to its beloved sister Republic in America the palms of the Marne and the Yser, of Verdun and the Somme. (Prolonged applause and cheers.)[1]

---

[1] At the close of this speech one of the deputies asked that the two speeches which the Chamber had just heard be issued as proclamations and read in the schools of France. There was no opposition and the proclamation was ordered.

AMERICA, A BEACON LIGHT OF PEACE

Gabriele D'Annunzio

For the soul of Italy to-day the capitol at Washington has become a beacon light. A Roman garland wreathes the bust dedicated to the hero whom free men call the glorious knight of humanity.

It is a garland pure as the branch of lilac offered by a poet on the bier of Lincoln. It is sacred as the ever flowering bough "with heart-shaped leaves of rich green." It seems as though in this April of passion and tempest there reëchoes the cry of that April, tense with joy and anguish, "O, captain! My captain, rise up! Hear the bells. Rise up, for your flag is flung."

Now the group of stars on the banner of the great republic has become a constellation of the spring, like Pleiades; a propitious sign to sailors, armed and unarmed alike; a spiritual token for all nations fighting a righteous war. I give the salute of Italy, of the Roman capitol, to the capitol at Washington; a salute to the people of the union, who now confirm and seal the pledge that liberty shall be preserved.

This Italian poet, who is now serving his country in the aviation corps, was "overcome with joy" on hearing of the entrance of the United States into the world war. This is his message cabled to America on Sunday morning, April 8, 1917.

Gabriele D'Annunzio, poet, novelist, and dramatist, was born in Pescara in 1864. He was educated at the College of Prato in Tuscany and at the University of Rome. He became a Member of the Italian Chamber in 1898.

To Italy alone of the allied nations the possibility was open of avoiding war and remaining a passive spectator. Italy took up arms gladly, less for the reconquest of her heritage than for the salvation of all the things which symbolize the grandeur of freedom. She armed herself, as to-day the American nation is arming herself, for the sake of an ideal. The spontaneous act consummated by the fellow-countrymen of Washington is a glorious sacrifice on behalf of the hopes of all mankind.

America has achieved a new birth. She has molded for herself a new heart. This is the miracle wrought by a righteous war, the miracle that unexpectedly to-day we of Italy see performed beyond an ocean dishonored by assassins and thieves.

Our war is not destructive. It is creative. With all manner of atrocities, all manner of shameful acts, the barbarian has striven to destroy the ideal which, until this struggle began, man had of man. The barbarian heaped upon the innocent, infamous outrages inspired by hate, alternating senile imprudence and brutal stupidity. The barbarian ground heroism to earth, cast down the airy cathedrals where congregated the aspirations of the eternal soul, burned the seats of wisdom decked with the flowers of all the arts; distorted the lineaments of Christ, tore off the garments of the Virgin.

Now once again we begin to have hope of the nobility of man. Love's face is radiant, though its eyes are moist with tears, for never was love so much beloved. Love overflows on all the world like a brook in May. Our hearts are not large enough to gather it and to hold it.

The people of Lincoln, springing to their feet to defend the eternal spirit of man, to-day increase immeasurably this sum of love opposed to fury, the fury of the barbarian.

"Ah! Liberty. Let others despair of thee. I will

never despair of thee," once cried your rugged poet. In this hope your nation arises to-day, in the north, south, east, west, to offer your strength, proclaiming our cause to be the noblest cause for which men have ever fought. You were an enormous and obtuse mass of riches and power; now you are transfigured into ardent, active spirituality. The roll of your drums drowns out the last wail of doubt.

April 15th is the anniversary of Lincoln's death. From his sepulcher there issue again the noble words which fell from his lips at Gettysburg, on soil sanctified by the blood of brave men. All your states, north, south, east, west, hear them. I say to you that "this nation, under God, shall have a new birth of freedom."

AMERICA ENTERS THE WAR

David Lloyd George

I AM the last man in the world, knowing for three years what our difficulties have been, what our anxieties have been, and what our fears have been — I am the last man in the world to say that the succor which is given from America is not in itself something to rejoice at, and to rejoice at greatly. But I also say that I value more the knowledge that America is going to win a right to be at the conference table when the terms of peace are discussed.

That conference will settle the destiny of nations and the course of human life for God knows how many years. It would have been a tragedy, a tragedy for mankind, if America had not been there, and there with all her influence and her power.

I can see peace, not a peace to be a beginning of war, not a peace which will be an endless preparation for strife and bloodshed, but a real peace. The world is an old world. You have never had the racking wars that have rolled like an ocean over Europe.

Europe has always lived under the menace of the sword. When this war began, two thirds of Europe was under autocratic rule. Now it is the other way about,

---

Before the American Luncheon Club of London, on April 12, 1917, Great Britain's Prime Minister spoke on the entrance of the United States into war with Germany.

Ambassador Page was present and responded for the Club. His speech follows this one.

DAVID LLOYD GEORGE

and democracy means peace. The democracy of France hesitated; the democracy of Italy hesitated long before it entered; the democracy of this country sprang back with a shudder and would never have entered that caldron had it not been for the invasion of Belgium; and if Prussia had been a democracy, there would have been no war.

Many strange things have happened in this war, aye, and stranger things will come, and they are coming rapidly. There are times in history when this world spins so leisurely along its destined course that it seems for centuries to be at a standstill. There are awful times when it rushes along at giddying pace, covering the track of centuries in a year. Those are the times we are living in now. Six weeks ago Russia was an autocracy. She now is one of the most advanced democracies in the world.

To-day we are waging one of the most devastating wars that the world has ever seen. To-morrow, to-morrow, not perhaps distant to-morrows, war may be abolished forever from the category of human crimes. This may be something like that fierce outburst of winter which we now are witnessing before we complete the time for the summer.

It is written of those gallant men who won that victory on Monday, from Canada, from Australia, and from this old country — it has proved that in spite of its age it is not decrepit — it is written of those gallant men that they attacked at dawn. Fitting work for the dawn — to drive out of forty miles of French soil those miscreants who had defiled her freedom. They attacked with the dawn. It is a significant phrase.

The great nations represented in the struggle for freedom — they are the heralds of dawn. They attacked with dawn, and those men are marching forward in the full radiance of that dawn, and soon Frenchmen and Americans, British and Russians, aye, Serbians, and Belgians, Montenegrins, and Roumanians, will emerge into the full light of a perfect day.

GREAT DAYS FOR THE REPUBLIC

WALTER HINES PAGE

THESE are great days for the republic. We have set out to help in an enterprise of saving the earth as a place worth living in.

There is no need to restate the meaning of this enterprise to you. What is new about it is that it now becomes our immediate American enterprise. The clear, solemn call of the President and the voice of Congress, which is the voice of the people, are to us the high call of duty. If there be an American in this room who has not volunteered to give any service that he can without thought of consequence or of pay, I don't see him.

From all of the states, from the states of the great Mississippi valley, from the South and from the Pacific, they will come, as many millions as need be. You are parts also of our great industrial organizations and financial institutions, and these, too, already are at the service of our government. We shall not have to do any commandeering.

Ambassador Page, representing the American Luncheon Club of London, made fitting reply to the words of Lloyd George in commending America on her newly taken stand on the side of the Allies.

Walter Hines Page is a North Carolinian by birth, having been born in that state on the 15th day of August, 1855. Mr. Page is well educated, having attended Randolph Macon College, and Tulane, Aberdeen (Scotland), and Johns Hopkins Universities. He became editor of *The Forum* in 1890, and of the *Atlantic Monthly* in 1896. He was editor of the *World's Work* when he was selected by President Wilson in 1913 to represent American interests at the Court of St. James.

For the first time we are coming to war in the old world — except, indeed, when once before we came thither to suppress the Barbary pirates. It is singular that our present errand is so similar.

Of our coming overseas many consequences will follow. First and foremost we trust for an earlier victory, and, secondly, for a better understanding of the United States by the free nations of Europe and of the free nations of Europe by the United States, and this, as I see it, is the largest constructive political need of the world.

We come in answer only to the high call of duty and not for any material reward; not for territory, not for indemnity or conquest, not for anything save the high duty to succor democracy when it is desperately assailed. We come only for the ideal; that is, the republic.

What is the United States? It is a vast territory of great resources and a hundred million prosperous people, yes, but more. The republic is a system of society, a scheme of life, a plan of freedom, a state of mind — an ideal that every human shall have the utmost possible opportunity for individual development and that nothing shall be put in the way of that development. It was for this and upon this that our fathers established it. This we haven't forgotten, nor shall we ever forget. It is to make sure that this ideal shall not now perish from the earth that brings the United States into this war. High as the cost and great as the toll may be, we shall be better for standing where we have always stood, whatever the cost.

COMRADES IN A COMMON CAUSE

BISHOP BRENT

WE comrades in the common cause have come together like sturdy Judas Maccabæus and his fellow patriots in the ancient story, to commit our decision to the Lord and place ourselves in His hands before we pitch our camp and go forth to battle. It were an unworthy cause that we could not commit to God with complete confidence. To-day we have this confidence.

This, I venture to say, is not merely the beginning of a new era, but of a new epoch. At this moment a great nation well skilled in self-sacrifice, is standing by with deep sympathy and bidding Godspeed to another great nation that is making its act of self-dedication to God. That altar upon which we Americans are to-day laying

---

On April 20, 1917, the British Government and people celebrated the entry of America into the world war. A historic service was held in St. Paul's Cathedral, London. The cathedral holds about 31,000 people and was filled to its farthest recesses, when King George and Queen Mary entered, followed by the mayors and aldermen of the twenty-six boroughs of London, wearing their scarlet robes of office.

The king and queen and Princess Mary were received at the west entrance by the lord mayor and sheriff, the archbishop of Canterbury, the dean and chapter of St. Paul's, and the United States ambassador, Walter Hines Page.

The American embassy and consular staffs occupied front seats with representatives of the Pilgrims, the American Society, the American Luncheon Club, and the American Chamber of Commerce. In the diplomatic section were officers in the uniforms of France, Russia, Italy, Belgium, Serbia, Montenegro, Roumania, and Japan.

The most impressive feature of the service came when the band played a stanza of "The Star-spangled Banner" and the great crowd rose as one man.

The sermon here given was preached by Bishop Brent, Episcopal bishop of the Philippines, from the text in Maccabees II. 13 ending, "having given out to his men the watchword, 'Victory is God's.'"

our lives and our fortunes is already occupied. After three years Great Britain and her allies have been fighting not merely for their own laws, their own homes, their liberty, and all they hold sacred, but for the great commonwealth of mankind.

To-day, when the United States avow their intention of giving themselves wholeheartedly to this great cause, the battle for the right assumes new proportions. A new power and victory — aye, a victory that is God's — is in sight. We Americans have never been oblivious to the fact that the people of this country have been standing for the same principles which we love and for which we live. England, thank God, is the mother of democracy, and England's children come back to-day to pour all their experience, the experience of a century and a half of independent life, with gratitude at the feet of their mother.

To-day we stand side by side with our fellows as common soldiers in the common fight. There have been great quarrels in the past that were results of misunderstanding, but our quarrel with Germany is not based on misunderstanding. It is due to understanding. Just as it was understanding that made us break with Germany, so it is understanding which makes us take our place by the side of the Allies. It would have been impossible for us to do otherwise.

This act of America has enabled her to find her soul. America, which stands for democracy, must champion the cause of the plain people at all costs. The plain people most desire peace. That is what America with the Allies is fighting for. She thinks so much of peace that she is ready to pay the cost of war. Our war to-day is that we may destroy war. One thing to do with war is to hunt it to its death and, please God, in this war we shall achieve our purpose.

RENÉ RAPHAEL VIVIANI

FRANCE GIVES YOU GREETING

René Viviani

I am indeed happy to have been chosen to present the greetings of the French Republic to the illustrious man whose name is in every French mouth to-day, whose incomparable message is at this very hour being read and commented upon in all our schools as the most perfect charter of human rights, and which so fully expresses the virtues of your race — long-suffering patience before appealing to force, and force to avenge that long-suffering patience when there can be no other means.

Since you are here to listen to me, I ask you to repeat a thousandfold the expression of our deep gratitude for the enthusiastic reception the American people have granted us in Washington. It is not to us, but to our beloved and heroic France, that reception was accorded. We were proud to be her children in those unforgetable moments when we read in the radiance of the faces we saw, the noble sincerity of your hearts. And I desire to thank also the press of the United States, represented by you. I fully realize the ardent and disinterested help you have given by your tireless propaganda in the cause of right. I know your action has been incalculable. Gentlemen, I thank you.

We have come to this land to salute the American

Soon after his arrival in America, April 27, 1917, as head of the French Government's Commission, M. Viviani gave this statement to newspaper men.

people and its Government, to call to fresh vigor our life-long friendship, sweet and cordial in the ordinary course of our lives, and which these tragic hours have raised to all the ardor of brotherly love — a brotherly love which in these last years of suffering has multiplied its most touching expressions. You have given help not only in treasure, in every act of kindness and good will, but for us your children have shed their blood, and the names of your sacred dead are inscribed forever in our hearts. And it was with a full knowledge of the meaning of what you did that you acted. Your inexhaustible generosity was not the charity of the fortunate to the distressed, it was an affirmation of your conscience, a reasoned approval of your judgment.

Your fellow-countrymen knew that under the savage assault of a nation of prey which has made of war, to quote a famous saying, its national industry, we were upholding with our incomparable allies — faithful and valiant to the death, with all those who are fighting shoulder to shoulder with us on the firing line, the sons of indomitable England — a struggle for the violated rights of man, for that democratic spirit which the forces of autocracy were attempting to crush throughout the world. We are ready to carry that struggle on to the end.

And now, as President Wilson has said, the Republic of the United States rises in its strength as a champion of right and rallies to the side of France and her allies. Only our descendants, when time has removed them sufficiently far from present events, will be able to measure the full significance, the grandeur of an historic act which has sent a thrill through the whole world. From to-day on all the forces of freedom are let loose. And not only victory, of which we were already assured, is certain; the true meaning of victory is made manifest. It cannot be merely a fortunate military conclusion to this struggle; it will be the victory of morality and right, and will forever secure the existence of a world in which all our children shall draw free breath in full peace and undisturbed pursuit of their labors.

THE FLAG ON THE FIRING LINE

THEODORE ROOSEVELT

I COME here to-night to appeal to the people of the great west, the people of the Mississippi valley, the people who are the spiritual heirs of the men who stood behind Lincoln and Grant.

You men and women who live beside the Great Lakes and on the lands drained by the Ohio, the Mississippi, and the Missouri have always represented what is most intensely American in our national life. When once waked up to actual conditions you have always stood with unfaltering courage and iron endurance for the national honor and the national interest.

I appeal to the sons and daughters of the men and women of the Civil War, to the grandsons and grand-daughters of the pioneers; I appeal to the women as much as to the men, for our nation has risen level to every great crisis only because in every such crisis the courage of its women flamed as high as the courage of the men.

I appeal to you to take the lead in making good the President's message of the 2nd of this month, in which he

---

Mr. Roosevelt delivered this speech to a crowd of some thirteen thousand people at the Chicago Stockyards Pavilion, when he visited that city on April 28, 1917, in the interest of the preparedness cause.

Former President Roosevelt was born in New York, October 27, 1858. After graduating from Harvard, he entered politics and was elected to the State Legislature in 1882. In 1898 he was the popular choice for governor in the Empire state. He was elected to the Vice Presidency of the United States under McKinley and after his (Mc-Kinley's) assassination on September 14, 1901, succeeded to the Presidency. Mr. Roosevelt was again made President in 1904.

set forth the reasons why it was our unescapable duty to make war upon Germany. It rests with us — with the American people — to make that message one of the great state documents of our history.

Let us accept the lessons it teaches. Let us grasp what it says as to the frightful wrongs Germany has committed upon us and upon the weaker nations of mankind, and the damage she has wrought to the whole fabric of civilization and of international good faith and morality.

Then let us steel our hearts and gird our loins to show that we are fit to stand among the free people whose freedom is buttressed by their self-reliant strength. Let us show by our deeds that we are fit to be the heirs of the men who founded the republic, and of the men who saved the republic; of the continentals who followed Washington, and of the men who wore the blue under Grant and the gray under Lee.

But, mind you, the message, the speech, will amount to nothing unless we make it good; and it can be made good only by the high valor of our fighting men, and by the resourceful and laborious energy of the men and women who, with deeds, not merely words, back up the fighting men.

We read the Declaration of Independence every Fourth of July because, and only because, the soldiers of Washington made that message good by their blood during the weary years of war that followed. If, after writing the Declaration of Independence, the men of '76 had failed with their bodies to make it good, it would be read now only with contempt and derision.

Our children still learn how Patrick Henry spoke for the heart of the American people when he said, "Give me liberty or give me death," but this generation is thrilled by his words only because the Americans of those days showed in very fact that they were ready to accept death rather than lose their liberty.

In Lincoln's deathless Gettysburg speech and second inaugural he solemnly pledged the honor of the American people to the hard and perilous task of preserving the union and freeing the slaves.

The pledge was kept. The American people fought to a finish the war which saved the union and freed the slave. If Lincoln and the men and women behind him had wavered, if they had grown faint-hearted and had shrunk from the fight, or had merely paid others to fight for them, they would have earned for themselves and for us the scorn of the nations of mankind.

The words of Lincoln will live forever only because they were made good by the deeds of the fighting men.

So it is now. We can make the President's message of April 2nd stand among the great state papers in our history; but we can do so only if we make the message good; and we can make it good only if we fight with all our strength now, at once; if at the earliest possible moment we put the flag on the firing line and keep it there, over a constantly growing army, until the war closes by a peace which brings victory to the great cause of democracy and civilization, the great cause of justice and fair play among the peoples of the world.

THEODORE ROOSEVELT

THE RIGHTS OF MANKIND

THEODORE ROOSEVELT

WE fight for our own rights. We fight for the rights of mankind. This great struggle is fundamentally a struggle for the fundamentals of civilization and democracy. The future of the free institutions of the world is at stake. The free people who govern themselves are lined up against the governments which deny freedom to their people.

Our cause is the cause of humanity. But we also have bitter wrongs of our own which it is our duty to redress. Our women and children and unarmed men, going about their peaceful business, have been murdered on the high seas, not once, but again and again and again.

With brutal insolence, after having for well-nigh two years persevered in this policy, Germany has announced that she will continue it, at our expense and at the expense of other neutrals, more ruthlessly than ever.

The injury thus done to us as a nation is as great as the injury done to a man if a ruffian slaps his wife's face. In such case, if the man is a man, he does not wait and hire somebody else to fight for him; and it would be an evil thing, a lasting calamity to this country, if the war ended, and found us merely preparing an army in safety at home, without having sent a man to the firing line; merely having paid some billions of dollars to other people so that with the bodies of their sons and brothers they might keep us in safety.

From a speech delivered in Chicago, April 28, 1917.

I ask that we send a fighting force over to the fighting line at the earliest possible moment, and I ask it in the name of our children and our children's children, so that they may hold their heads high over the memory of what this nation did in the world's great crisis.

I ask it for reasons of national morality no less than for our material self-interest. I ask it for the sake of our self-respect, our self-esteem.

Our children will have to read the history of what we have done during this war. Let us make the chapter that yet remains to be written one that our children shall read with pride; and they will read it only with a feeling of self-abasement, unless they read that in the times that tried men's souls we have shown valor and endurance and proud indifference to life when the honor of the flag and the welfare of mankind were at stake.

Put the flag on the firing line, and valiant men behind it; and keep it there, sending over a constantly growing stream of valiant men to aid those who have first gone.

In the Civil War there were many men who went to the front to pay with their bodies for the high faith of their souls. There were some men who hired others to go as substitutes to the front. Which ones among these men are the ones to whom we look back with pride — those who faced the bullets or those who paid with dollars to buy the willingness and ability of other men to fight? There is no need to answer.

In exactly the same way there should be no need to answer now the question as to whether we are merely to spend billions of dollars to help others fight, or to stand in the fighting line ourselves.

By all means spend the money. A prime essential is to furnish the Allies all the cargo ships they need for food and all the craft they need to help hunt down the submarines. By all means aid them with food and ships and money, and speedily; but do not stop there.

Show that we can fight, as well as furnish dollars and vegetables to fighting men. At the earliest possible moment send an expeditionary force abroad, show our German foes and our allied friends that we are in this war in deadly earnest, that we have put the flag on the firing line, and that we shall steadily increase the force behind that flag to any limit necessary in order to bring the peace of victory in this great contest for democracy, for civilization, and for the rights of free peoples.

AT THE TOMB OF WASHINGTON

M. Viviani and Mr. Balfour

René Viviani

We could not remain longer in Washington without accomplishing this pious pilgrimage. In this spot lies all that is mortal of a great hero. Close by this spot is the modest abode where Washington rested after the tremendous labor of achieving for a nation its emancipation. In this spot meet the admiration of the whole world and the veneration of the American people. In this spot rise before us the glorious memories left by the soldiers of France, led by Rochambeau and Lafayette; a descendant of the latter, my friend M. Chambrun, accompanies us. I esteem it an honor as well as satisfaction for my conscience to be entitled to render this homage to our ancestors in the presence of my colleague and friend, Mr. Balfour, who so nobly represents his

On April 30, 1917, representatives of the three great democracies paid homage to America's soldier and statesman at the tomb of Washington, and pledged themselves, each to the other, in the name of the dead to prosecute the present mighty struggle against autocracy on the lines he himself had followed in bringing America into being.

The British laid upon the tomb a wreath bearing the inscription given at the end of Mr. Balfour's peech.

A bronze palm such as France gives to her soldier dead was laid on the tomb by French privates, and General Joffre, the hero of the Marne, said, "In the French Army all venerate the name and memory of Washington. I respectfully salute here the great soldier and lay upon his tomb the palm we offer our soldiers who have died for their country."

M. Viviani, Minister of Justice and former premier of France, advanced before the tomb and delivered this address.

great nation. By thus coming to lay here the respectful tribute of every English mind, he shows in this historic moment of communion, what France has willed, what nations that live for liberty can do.

When we contemplate in the distant past the luminous presence of Washington, in nearer times the majestic figure of Abraham Lincoln, when we respectfully salute President Wilson, the worthy heir of these great memories, we at one glance measure the vast career of the American people. It is because the American people proclaimed and won for the nation the right to govern itself; it is because it proclaimed and won the equality of all men, that the free American people at the hour marked by fate has been enabled with commanding force to carry its action beyond the seas; it is because it was resolved to extend its action still further that Congress was enabled to obtain, within the space of a few days, the vote of conscription, and to proclaim the necessity for a national army in the full splendor of civil peace.

In the name of France, I salute the young army which will share in our common glory.

While paying this supreme tribute to the memory of Washington, I do not diminish the effect of my words when I turn my thoughts to the memory of so many unnamed heroes. I ask you before this tomb to bow, in earnest meditation and all the fervor of piety, before all the soldiers of the allied nations who for nearly three years have been fighting under different flags for the same ideal. I beg you to address the homage of your hearts and souls to all the heroes, born to live in happiness, in the tranquil pursuit of their labors, in the enjoyment of all human affections, who went into battle with virile cheerfulness, and gave themselves up, not to death alone, but to the eternal silence that closes over those whose sacrifice remains unnamed, in the full knowledge that save for these who loved them their names would disappear with their bodies. Their monument is in our hearts. Not the living alone greet us here; the ranks of the dead themselves rise to surround the soldiers of liberty.

At this solemn hour in the history of the world, while saluting from this sacred mound the final victory of justice, I extend to the republic of the United States the greeting of the French republic.

Mr. Balfour

M. Viviani has expressed in most eloquent words the feelings which grip us all here to-day. He has not only paid a fitting tribute to a great statesman, but he has brought our thoughts most vividly down to the present. The thousands who have given their lives, French, Russian, Italian, Belgian, Serbian, Montenegrin, Roumanian, Japanese, and British, were fighting for what they believed to be the cause of liberty.

There is no place in the world where a speech for the cause of liberty would be better placed than here at the tomb of Washington. But as that work has been so adequately done by a master of oratory, perhaps you will permit me to read a few words prepared by the British mission for the wreath we are to leave here to-day.

"Dedicated by the British mission to the immortal memory of George Washington, soldier, statesman, patriot, who would have rejoiced to see the country of which he was by birth a citizen and the country which his genius called into existence, fighting side by side to save mankind from subjection to a military despotism."

OUR HERITAGE OF LIBERTY

René Viviani

Since I have been granted the supreme honor of speaking before the representatives of the American people, may I ask them first to allow me to thank this magnificent Capital for the welcome it has accorded us? Accustomed as we are in our own free land to popular manifestations, and though we had been warned by your fellow-countrymen who live in Paris of the enthusiasm burning in your hearts, we are still full of the emotion raised by the sights that awaited us.

I shall never cease to see the proud and stalwart men who saluted our passage; your women, whose grace adds fresh beauty to your city, their arms outstretched, full of flowers; and your children hurrying to meet us as if our coming were looked upon as a lesson for them — all with one accord acclaiming in our perishable persons immortal France.

And I predict there will be a yet grander manifestation on the day when your illustrious President, relieved from the burden of power, will come among us bearing the salute of the Republic of the United States to a free Europe, whose foundations from end to end shall be based on right.

It is with unspeakable emotion that we crossed the threshold of this legislative palace, where prudence and

---

This address was given before the United States Senate on May 1, 1917.

boldness meet, and that I address you, the first foreigner in the annals of America to speak in this hall which only a few days since resounded with the words of virile force.

You have set all the democracies of the world the most magnificent example. So soon as the common peril was made manifest to you, with simplicity and within a few short days you voted a formidable war credit and proclaimed that a formidable army was to be raised. President Wilson's commentary on his acts, which you made yours, remains in the history of free peoples the weightiest of lessons.

Doubtless you were resolved to avenge the insults offered your flag, which the whole world respected; doubtless through the thickness of these massive walls the mournful cry of all the victims that criminal hands hurled into the depths of the sea has reached and stirred your souls; but it will be your honor in history that you also heard the cry of humanity and invoked against autocracy the right of democracies.

And I can only wonder as I speak what, if they still have any power to think, are the thoughts of the autocrats who three years ago against us, three months ago against you, unchained this conflict.

Ah! doubtless they said among themselves that a democracy is an ideal government; that it showers reforms on mankind; that it can in the domain of labor quicken all economic activities, but that it cannot make war. And yet now we see the French Republic fighting in defense of its territory and the liberty of nations and opposing to the avalanche let loose by Prussian militarism the union of all its children, who are still capable of striking many a weighty blow.

And now we see England, far removed like you from conscription, who has also, by virtue of a discipline all accept, raised from her soil millions of fighting men. And we see other nations accomplishing the same act; and that liberty not only inflames all hearts, but coordinates and brings into being all needed efforts.

And now we see all America rise in the midst of peace and sharpen her weapons for the common struggle.

Together we will carry on that struggle, and when by force we have at last imposed military victory, our labors will not be concluded. Our task will be — I quote the noble words of President Wilson — to organize the society of nations.

I well know that our enemies, who have never seen before them anything but horizons of carnage, will never cease to jeer at so noble a design. Such has always been the fate of great ideas at their birth; and if thinkers and men of action had allowed themselves to be discouraged by skeptics, mankind would still be in its infancy and we should still be slaves. After material victory we will win this moral victory.

We will shatter the ponderous sword of militarism; we will establish guaranties for peace; and then we can disappear from the world's stage, since we shall leave, at the cost of our common sacrifice, the noblest heritage future generations can possess.

THE OLDEST FREE ASSEMBLIES

Arthur James Balfour

Will you permit me on behalf of my friends and myself to offer you my deepest and sincerest thanks for the rare and valued honor which you have done us by receiving us here to-day? We all feel the greatness of the honor, but I think to none of us can it come home so closely as to one who, like myself, has been for forty-three years in the service of a free assembly like your own.

I rejoice to think that a member, a very old member, I am sorry to say, of the British House of Commons has been received here to-day by this great sister assembly with such kindness as you have shown to me and to my friends.

Ladies and gentlemen, these two assemblies are the greatest and the oldest of the free assemblies now govern-

---

On May 5, 1917, the "House of Representatives was the scene of a great outbreak of patriotism and enthusiasm." For the first time in American history a British official spoke in the House. The President of the United States and the Justices of the Supreme Court were present, an additional mark of courtesy to the speaker.

The Right Honorable Arthur James Balfour was born in Scotland, July 25, 1848. He was educated at Cambridge and holds honorary degrees from ten or more great universities on the Continent. He became a member of Parliament in 1874 and held the Prime Minister's portfolio from 1902 to 1905.

In April, 1917, he was nominated to head the British Mission to the United States, with the object of establishing greater coöperation between the two countries in the prosecution of their war against Germany. At the time of his visit to America Mr. Balfour was Secretary of State for Foreign Affairs.

ARTHUR J. BALFOUR AND JOSEPH H. CHOATE

ing great nations in the world. The history of the two is very different. The beginnings of the British House of Commons go back to a dim historic past and its full rights and status have only been conquered and permanently secured after centuries of political struggle.

Your fate has been a happier one. You were called into existence at a much later stage of social development. You came into being complete and perfected, and all your powers determined and your place in the constitution secured beyond chance of revolution; but, though the history of these two great assemblies is different, each of them represents the great democratic principle to which we look forward as the security for the future peace of the world.

All of the free assemblies now to be found governing the great nations of the earth have been modeled either upon your practice or upon ours or upon both combined.

Mr. Speaker, the compliment paid to the mission from Great Britain by such an assembly and upon such an occasion is one not one of us is ever likely to forget; but there is something, after all, even deeper and more significant in the circumstances under which I now have the honor to address you than any which arise out of the interchange of courtesies, however sincere, between two great and friendly nations.

We all, I think, feel instinctively that this is one of the great moments in the history of the world, and that what is happening on both sides of the Atlantic represents the drawing together of great and free peoples for mutual protection against the aggression of military despotism.

I am not one of those — none of you are among those — who are such bad democrats as to say that democracies make no mistakes. All free assemblies have made blunders; sometimes they have committed crimes. Why is it then that we look forward to the spirit of free institutions, and especially among our present enemies, as one of the greatest guarantees of the future peace of the world? I will say to you, gentlemen, how it seems to me.

It is quite true that the people and the representatives of the people may be betrayed by some momentary gust of passion into a policy which they ultimately deplore, but it is only a military despotism of the German type that can, through generations, if need be, pursue steadily, remorselessly, unscrupulously, and appallingly the object of dominating the civilization of mankind.

And, mark you, this evil, this menace under which we are now suffering is not one which diminishes with the growth of knowledge and progress of material civilization, but on the contrary it increases with them.

When I was young, we used to flatter ourselves that progress inevitably meant peace, and that growth of knowledge was always accompanied as its natural fruit by the growth of good will among the nations of the earth. Unhappily we know better now, and we know there is such a thing in the world as a power which can, with unvarying persistence, focus all the resources of knowledge and of civilization into the one great task of making itself the moral and material master of the world.

It is against that danger that we, the free peoples of western civilization, have banded ourselves together.

It is in that great cause that we are going to fight and are fighting at this very moment side by side. In that cause we shall surely conquer; and our children will look back to this fateful date as the one from which democracies can feel secure that their progress, their civilization, their rivalry, if need be, will be conducted, not on German lines, but in the friendly and Christian spirit which really befits the age in which we live.

Mr. Speaker, ladies and gentlemen, I beg most sincerely to repeat again how heartily I thank you for the cordial welcome which you have given us to-day, and to repeat my profound sense of the significance of this unique meeting.

CHAMPIONS OF LIBERTY

PRINCE UDINE

THE VICE PRESIDENT

SENATORS, it will perhaps rejoice you hereafter to remember that within a very few days you have had the honor and pleasure of participating in three great historic scenes. For myself, I may say that I am very glad the distinguished visitors and myself both belong to posterity rather than to ancestry, for I have a historic recollection that some 1900 years ago the ancestors of these distinguished gentlemen were pursuing through the islands of Britain my ancestors, clad in sheepskin.

I am glad that I have lived in a time when the eagles of the Senate and people of Rome come in peace to visit the American eagle in the Senate of the United States. (Applause.)

History sometimes reverses itself and sometimes repeats itself. When Rome stood exclusively for power and sought to bring the habitable globe under her control, she never quite succeeded in conquering the Belgian people. Nineteen hundred years after that failure the Roman people have concluded that what Rome as the representative of power could not do, no other representative of power shall ever be permitted to do. (Applause.)

History repeats itself in another instance. When I

Given at the reception of the Italian Commission in the United States Senate on May 31, 1917. Mr. Marshall's speech is given as a happy introduction.

was trying to ascertain the history of this great people,
digging it out of the original, I learned, as I pronounce
it in the Hoosier vulgate, that one of the great Romans
closed each of his addresses in the Roman Senate with
this remarkable statement: "Ceterum censeo Cartha-
ginem esse delendam." History, I hope, again repeats
itself in that the people of the seven-hilled city beside the
yellow Tiber have resolved that for themselves and for
humanity the house of Hapsburg must be destroyed.
(Loud applause.)

It is my honor and my pleasure to present to you the
representative of the people of Italy, the Prince of Udine.
(Loud applause.)

ADDRESS BY PRINCE UDINE

Mr. President and gentlemen of the Senate, I consider
it a great honor for the mission of His Majesty, the King
of Italy, to be welcomed by the American Senate; it is
also a great honor for me, and a source of deep satisfaction,
to greet you on behalf of my country and to speak in
this glorious assembly, which has never forgotten the
noble traditions of democracy and the principles of
liberty, in the name of which it was constituted.

In this hour of danger, in which military absolutism is
threatening every one, there are nations that have forgotten old and new rivalries, and have united to defeat this menace to the common safety. We are in a
more fortunate position. Between the United States of
America and Italy there has never been any cause of
conflict. Therefore, in your history and in ours there is
no page which should be forgotten in this hour of brotherhood. In our present alliance we need not forget any
war, nor any rivalry, nor any strife. If nothing brings

men closer together than to fight for the same ideals, and to face the sufferings and the dangers of a great war for the cause of justice and of humanity, we must acknowledge that this new and closer union means for us a greater bond of sympathy and solidarity in addition to those which already linked us.

This long friendship without strife, this union without mistrust, this cloudless future, are enhanced by the fact that both our peoples are at war, not because of any imminent danger that threatened us, but to defend the same ideals of humanity and justice. (Applause.)

Your wars have been fought for independence and for liberty, and your heroes have been men such as George Washington, Thomas Jefferson, and Abraham Lincoln — human heroes, shining lights of the intellect, who looked with a kindly heart even upon their adversaries. (Applause.)

We, too, after having suffered greatly at the hands of foreign oppressors, have won liberty and independence; and our heroes, the men who gathered around Victor Emmanuel II, and gave Italy unity and freedom, were men such as Cavour, Garibaldi, Mazzini, champions of idealism, men who belonged to humanity rather than to their own country, pure glories of the world's democracy. (Applause.)

Italy, gentlemen of the Senate, entered into the war with aims equal to those which you pursue. Her territory had not been invaded, her insecure boundaries had not been violated. Our people understood that the sacrifice of free nations was the prelude to their own sacrifice, and that we could not remain indifferent without denying the very reasons of our existence. (Applause.)

Italy has suffered more than any other nation in Europe the horror of foreign domination, the martyrdom of invasion and pillage; and, therefore, she will never forget the principles which presided over her birth and which constitute her strength and her defense.

Italy wants the safety of her boundaries and her coasts, and she wants to secure herself against new aggressions. Italy wants to deliver from long-standing martyrdom populations of Italian race and language that have been persecuted implacably, and are nevertheless prouder than ever of their Italian nationality. (Applause.)

But Italy has not been and never will be an element of discord in Europe; and as she willed her own free national existence at the cost of any sacrifice, so she will contribute with all her strength to the free existence and development of other nations.

The mission of which I have the honor to be the head, and in which there are representatives of the Senate of the Kingdom, of the Chamber of Deputies, and members of the Government, desires to express through me the liveliest sympathy to the representatives of the American people. (Applause.)

The message of your President, as our sovereign has said, is worthy, by the nobility of its conceptions and the dignity of its form, to rank with the most inspiring pages in the history of ancient and immortal Rome. (Applause.) It was greeted with the enthusiasm of faith when it made clear the objects of the war and defined the aims of American action. Our soldiers, at the foot of the snowy Alps, amid the atrocious life of underground trenches; our sailors, defying the treacherous warfare of the submarines; the populations of France and of Belgium, suffering under the most cruel servitude, could not read it without a profound emotion.

By proclaiming that right is more precious than peace; that autocratic governments, supported by the force of

arms, are a menace to civilization; by affirming the
necessity of guaranteeing the safety of the world's democracies; by proclaiming the right of small nations to live
and to prosper, America has now, through the action of
her President, acquired a title of merit which history will
never forget.   (Applause.)

LIBERTY OR DEATH

Baron Moncheur

THE VICE PRESIDENT

Senators, since that far-off, unrecorded hour when our ancestors began their slow westward movement, unnumbered and unremembered, thousands have died upon the field of battle for love, for hate, for liberty, for conquest, as freemen or as slaves. Every note in the gamut of human passion has been written in the anvil chorus of war. Many have struck the redeeming blow for their own country, but few have unsheathed their swords without the hope of self-aggrandizement. It remained for little Belgium to write in the blood of her martyred sons and daughters a new page in the annals of diplomacy, to inscribe thereon that the dishonor of a people is the aggregate of the selfishness of its citizens; that the honor of a people is the aggregate of the self-sacrifice of its citizens; that treaties are made to be kept, not broken; that a people may dare to walk through "the valley of the shadow of death," touching elbows with their convictions, but that they dare not climb to the mountain tops of safety if thereby they walk over the dead bodies of their high ideals; that a people may safely die if thereby they can compel an unwilling world to toss upon their new-made graves the white lily of a blameless life.

Given at the reception of the Belgian Commission in the United States Senate, June 22, 1917. Mr. Marshall's introductory remarks are especially graceful.

Here, Senators, ends all I know, and here begins what I believe: Belgium shall arise. The long night of her weeping shall end; the morning of a day of joy shall break over her desolated homes, her devastated fields, and her profaned altars. When it breaks, humanity will learn that when mankind gambles with truth and honor and humanity, the dice of the gods are always loaded. (Applause.)

To me, in all profane history, there is no sadder, sweeter, sublimer character than Sidney Carton. Dreamer of dreams, he walked his lonely, only way. In all the history of nations there is no sadder, sweeter, sublimer story than the story of Belgium. Doer of deeds, she, too, has walked her lonely, only way — the via dolorosa that leads to duty, death, and glory. Out of the depths and across the deeps the representatives of the remnant of her people and the guardians of her honor have come to us this day.

I present to you the chairman of that mission, Baron Moncheur. (Applause.)

ADDRESS BY BARON MONCHEUR

Mr. President and gentlemen of the Senate, when some years ago I had the honor of representing the Government of my King in the United States, I often came to the Senate, where I listened with deep interest to the debates of your distinguished body. In those times I never thought that some day it would be my privilege to speak from this historic tribune.

When the Vice President was kind enough to ask me to address the Senate, I admit that at first I hesitated to accept his gracious invitation.

How should I dare to speak in this Chamber, which has resounded to the eloquence and wisdom of so many distinguished statesmen whose utterances from this tribune have changed the history of the world?

How should I venture to address this body to which the distinction, the talent, and the wisdom of its members have given a unique place among the legislative assemblies of the world?

If, gentlemen, I have finally succeeded in overcoming this natural hesitation, it is only because of my great desire to express, as well as my words will permit, the gratitude and admiration which the whole Belgian nation feels toward the American people and toward their Government.

You all know the unspeakable evils which have befallen my unfortunate country—the unprovoked invasion accompanied by a deliberate system of terror, the burning of many of our thriving cities and of innumerable villages, the massacre of thousands of our peaceful citizens, the pillage and devastation of our country.

Then followed the iron hand of foreign domination, enormous war contributions exacted from all the nine Provinces of Belgium, ruinous requisitions of all sorts from our people, the seizure of the raw material of industry, and even the theft of our machinery which was sent into the country of our enemy for his own use, so that now the silence of death reigns in our industrial centers which before had been the most active in Europe.

You also know, gentlemen, the way in which this régime of oppression has been carried out — eighty thousand Belgians condemned, in one year, to various penalties for having displeased the invader; as, for example, the noble burgomaster of Brussels, who has been in imprisonment for the past two years for trying to uphold the principle of civic liberty which for centuries has been so dear to all Belgians.

You have learned also of the deportation of our workmen into Germany — a crime the horrors of which, according to the opinion of one of your countrymen, should cause more indignation throughout the entire world than all the previous outrages against the sacred principles of justice and of humanity.

But Belgium, even in the midst of the terrible misfortunes which have been brought upon her by her fidelity to treaties and by respect for her plighted word, does not regret her decision, and there is not a single Belgian worthy of the name who does not now, as on the first day of war, approve the judgment of our Government that it is better to die, if need be, rather than to live without honor. Like Patrick Henry, all Belgians say, "Give me liberty or give me death." (Applause.)

This sentiment will be shared by all the citizens of the great American Nation, who responded with such enthusiasm and with such unanimity to the noble words of your President when, in terms which held the world spellbound, he proclaimed the imprescriptible right of justice over force.

The courage of my fellow-countrymen has been strengthened, also, by the sympathy for our misfortunes which has been manifested throughout your great land. American initiative has bestowed most generous help upon our starving population, and, in offering from this tribune the expression of gratitude of every Belgian heart, I wish also to render special homage to that admirable organization, the commission for relief in Belgium, which has done so much to save our people from starvation. (Applause.)

Yes, gentlemen, the sympathy of America gives us new courage; and while King Albert, who since the fateful day when our territory was violated, has remained steadfastly at the front, continues the struggle with indomitable energy at the head of our army intrenched upon the last strip of our soil that remains to us; while the Queen, that worthy companion of a great sovereign, expends her unceasing efforts to comfort and relieve the victims of battle, exciting enthusiasm by her contempt for the danger to which she exposes herself day by day; on the other side of the enemy's line of steel stands the Belgian people, bowed beneath the yoke but never conquered, maintaining its unshaken patriotism in spite of the seductions of the enemy as well as in spite of his iron rule; the Belgian people, a martyr whose courage is upheld by our great Cardinal Mercier, awaits silently in the sacred union of all parties the final hour of deliverance. (Great applause.)

That hour, gentlemen, will, I am convinced, be materially hastened by the powerful aid of the United States, and the time approaches when Belgium, restored to full and complete independence, both politically and economically, will be able to thank in a fitting manner all those who have aided her to emerge from the darkness of the tomb into the glorious light of a new life. (Prolonged applause.)

SLAVES OR FREEMEN?

Alexander Kerensky

Two months have elapsed since the birth of Russian freedom. I did not come here in order to greet you. Our greetings have been dispatched to your trenches long since. Your pains and your sufferings were one of the motives that precipitated the revolution. We could no longer endure the imbecile lavishness with which the old order spilled your blood. I believed throughout the two months that the only power which could save our country and lead her on the right path was the consciousness of responsibility for every word and every act of ours — a responsibility resting on every one of us. This belief I still hold.

Comrades, soldiers and officers, I well know what your feelings are there in the trenches, but I also know what is going on here. Possibly the time is near when we shall have to say to you, "We cannot give you all the bread which you have a right to expect of us and all the ammunition on which you have a right to depend"; but this will come about through no fault of those who two months ago assumed before the tribunal of history and the whole world the formal and official responsibility for the honor and glory of our country.

Spoken in May, 1917, to the representatives of the soldiers who came from the front to Petrograd. Kerensky, called Russia's "Man of the Hour," undertook for months the superhuman task of reconciling the discordant elements in "free Russia."

ALEXANDER KERENSKY

The situation of Russia at present is complex and difficult. The process of transformation from slavery to liberty does not, of course, assume the form of a parade. It is a difficult and painful work, full of misconceptions, mutual misunderstandings, which prepare a field for cowardice and bad faith, turning free citizens into human dust.

The time of isolated countries is past. The world has long since become one family, which is frequently torn asunder by internal struggles, but which is nevertheless bound together by strong ties — social, economic, and cultural.

Should we, as contemptible slaves, fail to organize into a strong nation, then a dark, sanguine period of internal strife will surely come, and our ideals will be cast under the heels of that despotic rule which holds that might is right and not that right is might. Every one of us, from the soldier to the minister, and from the minister to the soldier, can do whatever he pleases, but he must do it with eyes wide open, placing his devotion to the common ideal above all else.

Comrades, for years we have suffered in silence and were forced to fulfill duties imposed upon us by the old hateful might. You were able to fire on the people when the government demanded that of you. And how do we stand now? Now we can no longer hold out! What does it mean? Does it mean that free Russia is a nation of rebellious slaves? (Uneasiness all over the hall.)

Comrades, I can't — I don't know how I can tell the people untruths and conceal from them the truth!

I came to you because my strength was giving way, because I am no longer conscious of my previous courage. I no longer have the confidence that we are facing not rebellious slaves, but conscious citizens engaged in the creation of a new Russia and going about their work with an enthusiasm worthy of the Russian people.

They tell us that the front is no longer a necessity; fraternizing is going on there. Do they fraternize on the French front? No, comrades. If we fraternize, then why not fraternize on both sides? Have not the forces of our adversary been transported to the Anglo-French front? And has not the Anglo-French offensive been already halted? As far as we are concerned, there is no such thing as a Russian front; there is but one front, and that is an Allied front.

We are marching toward peace, and I should not be a member of the Provisional Government were it to disregard the will of the people as far as ending the war goes; but there are roads wide open and there are narrow, dark alleys, a stroll through which might cause one to lose both his life and honor. We want to hasten the end of this fratricidal war; but to this end we must march across the straight open road.

We are not an assembly of tired people; we are a nation. There are paths. They are long and complex. We are in need of an enormous amount of perseverance and calm. If we propose new war aims, then it behooves us to conduct ourselves so as to command the respect of both friend and foe. No one respects a weakling.

I regret that I did not die two months ago. I would have died then happy with the dream that a new life had been kindled in Russia; hopeful of a time when we could respect each other without resorting to the knout; hopeful that we could rule our Empire, but not as it was ruled by our former despots.

This is all, comrades, that I care to say. It is, of course, possible that I am mistaken. The diagnosis that I have made may turn out to be incorrect, but I think I am not so much in error as would appear to others. My diagnosis is: If we do not immediately realize the tragedy and hopelessness of the situation; if we do not concede that the immediate responsibility rests on all; if our political organism will not work as smoothly as a well-oiled mechanism, then all that we dreamed of, all to which we are striving, will be cast years back and possibly drowned in blood. I want to believe that we will find the solution for our problems, and that we will march forward along the bright and open road of democracy.

The moment has come when every one must search the depths of his conscience in order to realize whither he himself is going and whither he is leading those who, through the fault of the old government which held the people in darkness, regard every printed word as law. It is not difficult to play with this element, but the game is apt to be overplayed.

I came here because I believed in my right to tell the truth as I understand it. People who even under the old régime went about their work openly and without fear of death, those people, I say, will not be terrorized. The fate of our country is in our hands. The country is in great danger. We have sipped of the cup of liberty and we are somewhat intoxicated. But we are not in need of intoxication; we are in need of the greatest possible sobriety and discipline. We must enter history so that they may write on our graves: "They died, but they were never slaves."

AMERICA GREETS THE RUSSIAN REPUBLIC

Woodrow Wilson

We are fighting for the liberty, the self-government, and the undictated development of all peoples, and every feature of the settlement that concludes this war must be conceived and executed for that purpose. Wrongs must first be righted and then adequate safeguards must be created to prevent their being committed again. We ought not to consider remedies merely because they have a pleasing and sonorous sound. Practical questions can be settled only by practical means. Phrases will not achieve the result. Effective readjustments will, and whatever readjustments are necessary must be made.

But they must follow a principle, and that principle is plain. No people must be forced under sovereignty under which it does not wish to live. No territory must change hands except for the purpose of securing those who inhabit it a fair chance of life and liberty. No indemnities must be insisted on except those that constitute payment for manifest wrongs done. No readjustments of power must be made except such as will tend to secure the future peace of the world and the future welfare and happiness of its peoples.

And then the free peoples of the world must draw together in some common covenant, some genuine and practical coöperation that will in effect combine their

---

Delivered by Ambassador Francis to the Russian Government at Petrograd, June 11, 1917.

force to secure peace and justice in the dealings of nations with one another. The brotherhood of mankind must no longer be a fair but empty phrase; it must be given a structure of force and reality. The nations must realize their common life and effect a workable partnership to secure that life against the aggressions of autocratic and self-pleasing power.

For these things we can afford to pour out blood and treasure. For these are the things we have always professed to desire, and unless we pour out blood and treasure now and succeed, we may never be able to unite or show conquering force again in the great cause of human liberty. The day has come to conquer or submit. If the forces of autocracy can divide us, they will overcome us; if we stand together, victory is certain and the liberty which victory will secure. We can afford then to be generous, but we cannot afford then or now to be weak or to omit any single guaranty of justice and security.

THE VOICE OF AMERICAN LABOR

Samuel Gompers

The gravest crisis in the world's history is now hanging in the balance and the course which Russia will pursue may have a determining influence whether democracy or autocracy shall prevail. That democracy and freedom will finally prevail there can be no doubt in the minds of men who know, but the cost, the time lost, and the sacrifices which would ensue from lack of united action may be appalling. It is to avoid this that I address you. In view of the grave crisis through which the Russian people are passing we assure you that you can rely absolutely upon the whole-hearted support and coöperation of the American people in the great war against our common enemy, kaiserism. In the fulfilment of that cause the American government has the support of ninety-nine per cent of the American people, including the working class of both the cities and of the agricultural sections.

In free America as in free Russia the agitators for a peace favorable to Prussian militarism have been allowed to express their opinions, so that conscious and unconscious tools of the kaiser appear more influential than they really are. You should realize the truth of the situation. There are but few in America willing to allow kaiserism and its allies to continue their rule over those

President Samuel Gompers of the American Federation of Labor sent this message by cable to the Executive Committee of the Russian Council of Workmen's and Soldiers' Deputies, May 6, 1917.

Samuel Gompers

non-German peoples who wish to be free from their domination. Should we not protest against the pro-kaiser Socialist interpretation of the demand for "no annexation," namely, that all oppressed non-German peoples shall be compelled to remain under the domination of Prussia and her lackeys, Austria and Turkey? Should we not rather accept the better interpretation that there must be no forcible annexations, but that every people must be free to choose any allegiance it desires, as demanded by the council of workmen's and soldiers' deputies?

Like yourselves, we are opposed to all punitive and improper indemnities. We denounce the onerous punitive indemnities already imposed by the kaiser upon the people of Servia, Belgium, and Poland.

America's workers share the view of the council of workmen's and soldiers' deputies, that the only way in which the German people can bring the war to an early end is by imitating the glorious example of the Russian people, compelling the abdication of the Hohenzollerns and the Hapsburgs and driving the tyrannous nobility, bureaucracy, and the military caste from power.

Let the German Socialists attend to this and cease their false pretenses and underground plotting to bring about an abortive peace in the interest of kaiserism and the ruling class. Let them cease calling pretended "international" conferences at the instigation or connivance of the kaiser. Let them cease their intrigues to cajole the Russian and American working people to interpret your demand "no annexation, no indemnities," in a way to leave undiminished the prestige and the power of the German military caste.

Now that Russian autocracy is overthrown, neither the American government nor the American people apprehend that the wisdom and experience of Russia in the coming constitutional assembly will adopt any form of government other than the one best suited to her needs. We feel confident that no message, no individual emissary, and no commission has been sent or will be sent with authority to offer any advice whatever to Russia as to the conduct of her internal affairs. Any commission that may be sent will help Russia in any way that she desires to combat kaiserism, wherever it exists or may manifest itself.

Word has reached us that false reports of an American purpose and of American opinions contrary to the above statement have gained some circulation in Russia. We denounce these reports as the criminal work of desperate pro-kaiser propagandists circulated with the intent to deceive and to arouse hostile feelings between the two great democracies of the world. The Russian people should know that these activities are only additional manifestations of the "dark forces" with which Russia has been only too familiar in the unhappy past.

The American government, the American people, the American labor movement are whole-heartedly with the Russian workers, the Russian masses, in the great effort to maintain the freedom you have already achieved, and to solve the grave problems yet before you.

We earnestly appeal to you to make common cause with us to abolish all forms of autocracy and despotism, and to establish and maintain for generations yet unborn the priceless treasures of justice, freedom, democracy, and humanity.

A GRAVE SITUATION

AMBASSADOR BAKHMETIEFF

THE VICE PRESIDENT

SENATORS, the kaleidoscope of current history is being turned so rapidly that to the normal eye the combinations of yesterday are forgotten, of to-day are uncertain, and of to-morrow are unknown. And yet as from time to time there are unfolded in this most sacred and historic spot portions of the panorama of the greatest tragedy that has been enacted since Calvary there stands out one clear-cut central figure, the figure of the dauntless and undaunted man who dares to draw his sword either to preserve or to obtain for himself and for his fellows the right of self-government, the heritage of life, of liberty, and of the pursuit of happiness. It matters but little to us the feature and the form of that man, his lineage or his language, if he speak in the full and confident tones of a manhood, or in the lisping tongue of infantile possession of those rights. But if we hear from his lips the golden rule of statecraft, then he is our brother. He has a right to be, and he has a right to be here.

We are honored this day by the representatives of a people who have been our long-time and unvarying friends. It is not possible for me to think in the terms of

---

Spoken at the reception of the Russian Commission in the United States Senate, June 26, 1917. It was preceded by another of Mr. Marshall's graceful introductions.

countries and continents and governments. My mind thinks only in the terms of men; and perhaps this is as it should be, for the Goddess of Liberty is not always a strong and virile woman. In the hours of peace she becomes pale and anemic, and it is oftentimes necessary to keep her alive by transfusing into her veins the blood of patriotic and self-sacrificing men.

I cannot think of France, of England, of Italy, of America; I think only of Viviani and Joffre, of Balfour and Haig, of Udine and Cadorna, of Wilson and Pershing. On this day as I look into the eyes, the storm-tossed eyes, of these our guests, I cannot think of Russia as the land of Alexander and Nicholas. She seems to me to be only the home of Kropotkin and of Tolstoi.

Travelers tell us that there is a point in Iceland where the rays of the setting and of the rising sun mingle. Already upon the far-flung eastern battle line of Europe the rays of the setting sun of autocracy have mingled with the rays of the rising sun of democracy. May that sun grow in light and warmth, and may it be undimmed by the clouds of internal dissension. May democracy everywhere understand that its first duty is to make a democrat a free man everywhere on earth. (Applause.)

Last week we went with little Belgium sadly to her Gethsemane; to-day let us go gladly, with mighty Russia, to her Mount of Transfiguration. (Applause.)

I present to you the chairman of this commission, Mr. B. A. Bakhmetieff.

ADDRESS BY AMBASSADOR BAKHMETIEFF

Mr. President and gentlemen of the Senate, at the outset permit me to express to you sincere thanks and keen appreciation for the warm reception you have so graciously given to the members of the mission and to myself. Great is the honor you have bestowed by permitting me to address your distinguished body, abrogating thus a custom which has been upheld for more than a century, but still more gratifying is the expression of cordial sympathy and friendly feeling which has been so manifestly exhibited by your reception.

That bonds of friendship and sympathy united the people of the two nations we knew before we departed from Russia. They were amply manifested during the early days of the revolution. The act of prompt recognition of our new Government has been of incalculable value. For the brotherly encouragement which you gave us, and for the noble manner in which you so generously stretched forth a helping hand, we are here, in behalf of the new Russia, to express to you our deepest and most heartfelt gratitude. (Applause.)

At this moment all eyes are turned on Russia. Many hopes and many doubts are raised by the tide of events in the greatest of revolutions at an epoch in the world's greatest war. Justifiable is the attention, lawful the hopes, and naturally conceivable the anxiety. The fate of nations, the fate of the world is at stake, all dependent on the fate of Russia. Freedom and peace will be the blessings of the future if Russia happily emerges from the struggle a powerful democracy, sparkling with the gallantry of her army returning from fields won in common strife with her allies. (Great applause.)

I am not going to conceal the gravity of the situation that confronts the Russian Provisional Government. The revolution called for the reconstruction of the very foundations of our national life. It is not easy to comprehend what it means to reorganize all of Russia on democratic lines. Such work involves the whole of our social, economic, and political relations. The entire State structure is affected by the changes, involving village, district, county; in fact, every part from the smallest to the central State. The creation anew of a country of boundless expanse on distinctly new principles will, of course, take time, and impatience should not be shown in the consummation of so grand an event as Russia's entry into the ranks of free nations.

There has been a period, closely following the revolution, of almost total suspension of all military activity, a period of what appeared to be disintegration of the army, a period which gave rise to serious doubts and to gloomy forebodings. At the same time there ensued unlimited freedom of speech and of the press, which afforded opportunities for expression of the most extreme and anti-national views, from all of which resulted widespread rumors throughout the world that Russia would abandon the war and conclude a separate peace with the central powers.

With all emphasis and with the deepest conviction, may I reiterate the statement that such rumors were wholly without foundation in fact. Russia rejects with indignation any idea of separate peace. (Prolonged applause.) What my country is striving for is the establishment of a firm and lasting peace between democratic nations. Russia is firmly convinced that a separate peace would mean the triumph of German autocracy, would render lasting peace impossible, create the greatest danger for democracy and liberty, and ever be a threatening menace to the new-born freedom of Russia. (Applause.)

Peaceful in its intentions, striving for a lasting peace based on democratic principles and established by democratic will, the Russian people and its army are rallying their forces around the banners of freedom, strengthening their ranks in cheerful self-consciousness; to die, but not to be slaves. (Great applause.)

Russia wants the world to be safe for democracy. To make it safe means to have democracy rule the world. (Prolonged applause.)

WHY ARE WE FIGHTING GERMANY?

Franklin K. Lane

Why are we fighting Germany? The brief answer is that ours is a war of self-defense. We did not wish to fight Germany. She made the attack upon us, not on our shores, but on our ships, our lives, our rights, our future. For two years and more we held to a neutrality that made us apologists for things which outraged man's common sense of fair play and humanity.

At each new offense — the invasion of Belgium, the killing of civilian Belgians, the attacks on Scarborough and other defenseless towns, the laying of mines in neutral waters, the fencing off of the seas — and on and on through the months we said: "This is war — archaic, uncivilized war, but war. All rules have been thrown away; all nobility. Man has come down to the primitive brute, and while we cannot justify we will not intervene. It is not our war."

Then why are we in? Because we could not keep out. The invasion of Belgium, which opened the war, led to the invasion of the United States, by slow, steady, logical steps. Our sympathies evolved into a conviction of self-interest. Our love of fair play ripened into alarm at our own peril.

And so we came into this war for ourselves. It is a war to save America, to preserve self-respect, to justify

---

This address was given by the Secretary of the Interior, before the Home Club of the Department of the Interior, Washington, D.C., June 4, 1917.

FRANKLIN K. LANE

our right to live as we have lived, not as some one else wishes us to live. In the name of freedom we challenge with ships and men, money and an undaunted spirit, that word "verboten" which Germany has written upon the sea and upon the land. For America is not the name of so much territory. It is a living spirit, born in travail, grown in the rough school of bitter experiences, a living spirit which has purpose and pride, knows why it wishes to live and to what end, knows how it comes to be respected by the world, and hopes to retain that respect by living on with the light of Lincoln's love of man as its old and new testament.

With this background of history and in this sense, then, we fight Germany:

Because of Belgium — invaded, outraged, enslaved, impoverished Belgium. We cannot forget Liége, Louvain, and Cardinal Mercier. Translated into terms of American history these names stand for Bunker Hill, Lexington, and Patrick Henry.

Because of France — invaded, desecrated France, a million of whose heroic sons have died to save the land of Lafayette. Glorious golden France, the preserver of the arts, the land of noble spirit. The first land to follow our lead into republican liberty.

Because of England — from whom came the laws, traditions, standards of life, and inherent love of liberty which we call Anglo-Saxon civilization. We defeated her once on the land and once upon the sea. But Australia, New Zealand, Africa, and Canada are free because of what we did. And they are with us in the fight for the freedom of the seas.

Because of Russia — new Russia. She must not be overwhelmed now. Not now, surely, when she is just born into freedom. Her peasants must have their chance;

they must go to school to Washington, to Jefferson, and to Lincoln, until they know their way about in this new, strange world of government by the popular will.

And because of other peoples, with their rising hope that the world may be freed from government by the soldier.

We are fighting Germany because she sought to terrorize us and then to fool us. We could not believe that Germany would do what she said she would do upon the seas.

We still hear the piteous cry of children coming up out of the sea where the *Lusitania* went down. And Germany has never asked forgiveness of the world.

We saw the *Sussex* sunk, crowded with the sons and daughters of neutral nations.

We saw ship after ship sent to the bottom — ships of mercy bound out of America for the starving Belgians; ships carrying the Red Cross and laden with the wounded of all nations; ships carrying food and clothing to friendly, harmless, terrorized peoples; ships flying the Stars and Stripes — sent to the bottom hundreds of miles from shore, manned by American seamen, murdered against all law, without warning.

We are fighting Germany because she violated our confidence. Paid German spies filled our cities. Officials of her government, received as the guests of this nation, lived with us to bribe and terrorize, defying our law and the law of nations.

We are fighting Germany because while we were yet her friend — the only great power that still held hands off, — she sent the Zimmermann note, calling to her aid Mexico, our southern neighbor, and hoping to lure Japan, our western neighbor, into war against this nation of peace.

We are fighting Germany because in this war feudalism

is making its last stand against oncoming democracy. We see it now. This is a war against an old spirit, an ancient, outworn spirit. It is a war against feudalism — the right of the castle on the hill to rule the village below. It is a war for democracy — the right of all to be their own masters. Let Germany be feudal if she will! But she must not spread her system over a world that has outgrown it. Feudalism plus science, thirteenth century plus twentieth — this is the religion of the mistaken Germany that has linked itself with the Turk — that has, too, adopted the method of Mahomet. "The state has no conscience." "The state can do no wrong." With the spirit of the fanatic she believes this gospel and that it is her duty to spread it by force.

With poison gas that makes living a hell, with submarines that sneak through the seas to murder slyly non-combatants, with dirigibles that bombard men and women while they sleep, with a perfected system of terrorization that the modern world first heard of when German troops entered China — German feudalism is making war upon mankind.

Let this old spirit of evil have its way and no man will live in America without paying toll to it in manhood and in money. This spirit might demand Canada from a defeated, navyless England, and then our dreams of peace on the north would be at an end. We would live, as France has lived for forty years, in haunting terror.

America speaks for the world in fighting Germany. Mark on a map those countries which are Germany's allies and you will mark but four, running from the Baltic through Austria and Bulgaria to Turkey. All the other nations, the whole globe around, are in arms against her or are unable to move. There is deep meaning in this.

We fight with the world for an honest world, in which nations keep their word; for a world in which nations do not live by swagger or by threat; for a world in which men think of the ways in which they can conquer the common cruelties of nature instead of inventing more horrible cruelties to inflict upon the spirit and body of man; for a world in which the ambition of the philosophy of a few shall not make miserable all mankind; for a world in which the man is held more precious than the machine, the system, or the state.

FREE FROM THE GERMAN YOKE

Max F. Meyer

I am thoroughly familiar with the present organization of the German social body and with its culmination, the present German government. I have lived in Germany twenty-five years. I was born there. I was educated there. I spent nineteen years of my life in German educational institutions, from the kindergarten to the research laboratory.

I confess that at the beginning of this war my sympathies were divided. The German nation had many justifiable complaints against its neighbors. But whatever wrongs the German nation may have suffered in the past from other nations, the German government during this war has had more than one opportunity to have them set right and to terminate the war. Its actions show that world domination, not justice, is its aim. I sympathize with the German people, but not with their government. Perhaps you would appreciate your American citizenship better if, like me, you had been born and brought up in Germany.

If Germany wins this war, fifty years hence its government will rule the American people. I do not want my American children to be put under the yoke which I escaped by coming to America.

From a letter from Professor Meyer of the University of Missouri to the People's Council of America for Democracy and Peace, August 13, 1917.

My hope is that the German government will be over-thrown and that the German nation, my relatives and friends, will enter an international organization for peace and justice. But the German government, this fearful danger to our future, can be overthrown only by raising armies, not by sitting around the council table and work-ing for the repeal of the conscription laws.

THE GERMAN–AMERICAN

Hans Zinsser

THERE are those among us who have been brought up in the best German tradition. They have been taught from childhood the literature and music of Germany. They have studied in her universities and have taken grateful pride in memories of their immediate forefathers. But all this has been ploughed under by the policy of merciless and materialistic efficiency with which a harsh and bureaucratic government has succeeded in hypnotizing a whole people.

Under these circumstances, who can have a stronger desire to see the German military power defeated than we? This is our '76. Perhaps we feel about it much as the colonists felt when they gathered about the arsenal in Concord. They were English far more than we are German, yet they fought because of their inherent sense of liberty. In the same way there are men and women of German lineage in this country who resent the policy of the present ruling German group much more than is possible for Americans of pure Anglo-Saxon blood. We are in this war, heart and soul, not only because our adopted country has declared war, not only because of Belgium, of Serbia, of the *Lusitania*, of the U-boats, of the Mexican plot — sufficient reasons in themselves — but in addition to all this we believe it is for us to redeem in as far as we may the blot upon the memories of our fathers.

Professor Hans Zinsser, who comes of old-fashioned German liberal stock, appeared at the opening of the Columbia University College of Physicians and Surgeons the other day wearing the uniform of a major in the United States army. His address explains. This is taken from the *Chicago Tribune* of October 1, 1917.

THE MENACE OF PRUSSIANISM

Otto H. Kahn

I SPEAK as one who has seen the spirit of the Prussian governing class at work from close by, having at its disposal and using to the full practically every agency for molding the public mind.

I have watched it proceed with relentless persistency and profound cunning to instil into the nation the demoniacal obsession of power-worship and world-dominion, to modify and pervert the mentality, indeed the very fiber and moral substance of the German people — a people which until misled, corrupted, and systematically poisoned by the Prussian ruling caste, was, and deserved to be, an honored, valued, and welcome member of the family of nations.

I have hated and loathed that spirit ever since it came within my ken many years ago, hated it all the more as I saw it ruthlessly pulling down a thing which was dear to me, the old Germany to which I was linked by ties of blood, by fond memories and cherished sentiments.

The difference in the degree of guilt as between the German people and their Prussian or Prussianized rulers and leaders, for the monstrous crime of this war and the atrocious barbarism of its conduct, is the difference be-

This address was made in late September, 1917, before the Chamber of Commerce at Harrisburg, Pa. Mr. Kahn is a member of the banking firm of Kuhn, Loeb & Co. He is of German parentage, but his sentiments are those of millions of loyal German-Americans throughout the whole country.

tween the man who, acting under the influence of a poisonous drug, runs amuck in mad frenzy, and the unspeakable malefactor who administered that drug, well knowing and fully intending the ghastly consequences which were bound to follow.

The world fervently longs for peace. But there can be no peace answering to the true meaning of the word, no peace permitting the nations of the earth, great and small, to walk unarmed and unafraid, until the teaching and the leadership of the apostles of an outlaw creed shall have become discredited and hateful in the sight of the German people, until that people shall have awakened to a consciousness of the unfathomable guilt of those whom they have followed into calamity and shame, until a mood of penitence and of a decent respect for the opinions of mankind shall have supplanted the sway of what President Wilson has so trenchantly termed "truculence and treachery."

God grant that the German people may before long work out their own salvation and find the only road which will give to the world an early peace and lead Germany back into the family of nations from which it is now an outcast.

From each of my visits to Germany for twenty-five years, I came away more appalled by the sinister transmutation Prussianism had wrought amongst the people, and by the portentous menace I recognized in it for the entire world.

It had given to Germany unparalleled prosperity, beneficent and advanced social legislation, and not a few other things of value, but it had taken in payment the soul of the race. It had made a "devil's bargain."

And when this war broke out in Europe, I knew that the issue had been joined between the powers of brutal might and insensate ambition on the one side and the forces of humanity and liberty on the other, between darkness and light.

Many there were at that time — and amongst them men for whose character I had high respect and whose motives were beyond any possible suspicion — who said their own and America's duty was strict neutrality, mentally and actually, but personally I believed from the beginning of the war, whether we liked all the elements of the Allies' combination or not — and I certainly did not like the Russia of the Czars — that the cause of the Allies was America's cause.

I believed that this was no ordinary war between peoples for a question of national interest or even national honor, but a conflict between fundamental principles and ideas; and so believing, I was bound to feel that the natural lines of race, blood, and kinship could not be the determining lines for one's attitude and alignment, but that each man, whatever his origin, had to decide according to his judgment and conscience on which side was the right and on which was the wrong and take his stand accordingly, whatever the wrench and anguish of the decision. And thus I took my stand three years ago.

But whatever one's views and feelings, whatever the country of one's birth or kin, only one course was left for all those claiming the privilege of American citizenship when by action of the President and Congress the cause and the fight of the Allies was formally made our cause and our fight. The duty of loyal allegiance and faithful service to his country, even unto death, rests, of course, upon every American.

But if it be possible to speak of a comparative degree concerning what is the highest as it is the most elementary attitude of citizenship, that duty may almost be said to rest with an even more solemn and compelling obligation upon Americans of foreign origin than upon native Americans. For we Americans of foreign antecedents are here not by the accidental right of birth, but by our own free choice for better or for worse.

We are your fellow-citizens because you accepted our oath of allegiance as given in good faith, and because you have opened to us in generous trust the portals of American opportunity and freedom, and you have admitted us to membership in the family of Americans, giving us equal rights in the great inheritance which has been created by the blood and the toil of your ancestors, asking nothing from us in return but decent citizenship and adherence to those ideals and principles which are symbolized by the glorious flag of America.

Woe to the foreign-born American who betrays the splendid trust which you have reposed in him! Woe to the German-American, so-called, who, in this sacred war for a cause as high as any for which ever people took up arms, does not feel a solemn urge, does not show an eager determination to be in the very forefront of the struggle, does not prove a patriotic jealousy, in thought, in action, and in speech, to rival and to outdo his native-born fellow-citizen in devotion and in willing sacrifice for the country of his choice and adoption and sworn allegiance and of their common affection and pride.

As Washington led Americans of British blood to fight against Great Britain, as Lincoln called upon Americans of the North to fight their very brothers of the South, so Americans of German descent are now summoned to join in our country's righteous struggle against a people of their own blood which, under the evil spell of a dreadful obsession, and, Heaven knows, through no fault of ours, has made itself the enemy of this peace-loving nation, as it is the enemy of peace and right and freedom throughout the world.

To gain America's independence, to defeat oppression and tyranny, was indeed to gain a great cause. To defend the very foundations of liberty and humanity, the very groundwork of fair dealing between nations, the very basis of peaceable living together among the peoples of the earth against the fierce and brutal onslaught of ruthless, lawless, faithless might; to spend the lives and the fortunes of this generation so that our descendants may be freed from the dreadful calamity of war and the fear of war, so that the energies and millions and billions of treasure now devoted to plans and instruments of destruction may be given henceforth to fruitful works of peace and progress and to the betterment of the conditions of the people — that is the highest cause for which any people ever unsheathed its sword.

THE BASIS FOR ENDURING PEACE

WOODROW WILSON

EVERY heart that has not been blinded and hardened by this terrible war must be touched by this moving appeal of his Holiness the Pope; must feel the dignity and force of the humane and generous motives which prompted it, and must fervently wish that we might take the path of peace he so persuasively points out. But it would be folly to take it if it does not in fact lead to the goal he proposes.

Our response must be based upon the stern facts, and upon nothing else. It is not a mere cessation of arms he desires; it is a stable and enduring peace. This agony must not be gone through with again, and it must be a matter of very sober judgment what will insure us against it.

His Holiness, in substance, proposes that we return to the *status quo ante bellum*, and that then there be a general condonation, disarmament, and a concert of nations based upon an acceptance of the principle of arbitration; that by a similar concert freedom of the seas be established, and that the territorial claims of France and Italy, the perplexing problems of the Balkan states, and the restitution of Poland be left to such conciliatory adjustments as may be possible in the new temper of such a peace, due regard being paid to the aspirations of

---

Reply of President Wilson to the peace note of Pope Benedict XV, signed, as is customary, by the Secretary of State.

the peoples whose political fortunes and affiliations will be involved.

It is manifest that no part of this program can be successfully carried out unless the restitution of the *status quo ante* furnishes a firm and satisfactory basis for it.

The object of this war is to deliver the free peoples of the world from the menace and the actual power of a vast military establishment controlled by an irresponsible government which, having secretly planned to dominate the world, proceeded to carry the plan out without regard either to the sacred obligations of treaty or the long established practices and long cherished principles of international action and honor; which chose its own time for the war, delivered its blow fiercely and suddenly, stopped at no barrier either of law or of mercy, swept a whole continent within the tide of blood — not the blood of soldiers only but the blood of innocent women and children also, and of the helpless and the poor — and now stands, balked but not defeated, the enemy of four fifths of the world.

This power is not the German people. It is the ruthless master of the German people. It is no business of ours how that great people came under its control or submitted with temporary zest to the domination of its purpose, but it is our business to see to it that the history of the rest of the world is no longer left to its handling.

To deal with such a power by way of peace, upon the plan proposed by his Holiness the Pope, would, so far as we can see, involve a recuperation of its strength and a renewal of its policy; would make it necessary to create a permanent hostile combination of nations against the German people, who are its instruments, and would result in abandoning the new-born Russia to the intrigue, the manifold subtle interference, and the certain counterrevolution, which would be attempted by all the malign influences to which the German government has of late accustomed the world.

Can peace be based upon a restitution of its power or upon any word of honor it could pledge in a treaty of settlement and accommodation?

Responsible statesmen must now everywhere see, if they never saw before, that no peace can rest securely upon political or economic restriction meant to benefit some nations and cripple or embarrass others, upon vindictive action of any sort, or any kind of revenge or deliberate injury.

The American people have suffered intolerable wrongs at the hands of the Imperial German government, but they desire no reprisal upon the German people, who have themselves suffered all things in this war, which they did not choose. America believes that peace should rest upon the rights of peoples, not the rights of governments — the rights of peoples great or small, weak or powerful — their equal right to freedom and security and self-government and to a participation upon fair terms in the economic opportunities of the world — the German people of course included, if they will accept equality and not seek domination.

The test, therefore, of every plan of peace is this: Is it based upon the faith of all the peoples involved, or merely upon the word of an ambitious and intriguing government on the one hand and a group of free peoples on the other? This is the test which goes to the root of the matter; and it is the test which must be applied.

The purposes of the United States in this war are known to the whole world — to every people to whom the truth has been permitted to come. They do not need to be stated again. We seek no material advantage of any kind. We believe that the intolerable wrongs done in this war by the furious and brutal power of the Imperial German government ought to be repaired, but not at the expense of the sovereignty of any people — rather a vindication of the sovereignty both of those that are weak and of those that are strong.

Punitive damages, the dismemberment of empires, the establishment of selfish and exclusive economic leagues, we deem inexpedient and in the end worse than futile, no proper basis for a peace of any kind, least of all for an enduring peace. That must be based upon justice and fairness and the common rights of mankind.

We cannot take the word of the present rulers of Germany as a guaranty of anything that is to endure, unless explicitly supported by such conclusive evidence of the will and purpose of the German people themselves as the other peoples of the world would be justified in accepting.

Without such guaranties, treaties of settlement, agreements for disarmament, covenants to set up arbitration in the place of force, territorial adjustments, reconstitutions of small nations, if made with the German government, no man, no nation, could now depend on.

We must await some new evidence of the purposes of the great peoples of the central powers.

God grant it may be given soon and in a way to restore the confidence of all peoples everywhere in the faith of nations and the possibility of a covenanted peace.

AMERICA'S CONDITIONS FOR PEACE

Woodrow Wilson

Gentlemen of the Congress: Once more, as repeatedly before, the spokesmen of the Central Empires have indicated their desire to discuss the objects of the war and the possible basis of a general peace. Parleys have been in progress at Brest-Litovsk between Russian representatives and representatives of the Central Powers, to which the attention of all the belligerents has been invited for the purpose of ascertaining whether it may be possible to extend these parleys into a general conference with regard to terms of peace and settlement.

The Russian representatives presented not only a perfectly definite statement of the principles upon which they would be willing to conclude peace, but also an equally definite program of the concrete application of those principles. The representatives of the Central Powers, on their part, presented an outline of settlement which, if much less definite, seemed susceptible of liberal interpretation until their specific program of practical terms was added.

That program proposed no concessions at all, either to the sovereignty of Russia or to the preferences of the populations with whose fortunes it dealt, but meant, in a word, that the Central Empires were to keep every foot of territory their armed forces had occupied — every province, every city, every point of vantage — as a permanent addition to their territories and their power.

This message, delivered before the Congress, January 8, 1918, is considered to state definitely the war aims of the Allies.

It is a reasonable conjecture that the general principles of settlement which they at first suggested originated with the more liberal statesmen of Germany and Austria, the men who have begun to feel the force of their own people's thought and purpose, while the concrete terms of actual settlement came from the military leaders, who have no thought but to keep what they have. The negotiations have been broken off. The Russian representatives were sincere and in earnest. They cannot entertain such proposals of conquest and domination.

The whole incident is full of significance. It is also full of perplexity. With whom are the Russian representatives dealing? For whom are the representatives of the Central Powers speaking? Are they speaking for the majorities of their respective Parliaments or for the minority parties, that military and imperialistic minority which has so far dominated their whole policy and controlled the affairs of Turkey and of the Balkan states which have felt obliged to become their associates in this war?

The Russian representatives have insisted, very justly, very wisely and in the true spirit of modern democracy, that the conferences they have been holding with the Teutonic and Turkish statesmen should be held with open, not closed doors, and all the world has been audience, as was desired. To whom have we been listening, then? To those who speak the spirit and intention of the resolutions of the German Reichstag of the 9th of July last, the spirit and intention of the liberal leaders and parties of Germany, or to those who resist and defy that spirit and intention and insist upon conquest and subjugation?

Or are we listening, in fact, to both, unreconciled and in open and hopeless contradiction? These are very serious and pregnant questions. Upon the answer to them depends the peace of the world.

But whatever the results of the parleys at Brest-Litovsk, whatever the confusions of counsel and of purpose in the utterances of the spokesmen of the Central Empires, they have again attempted to acquaint the world with their objects in the war, and have again challenged their adversaries to say what their objects are and what sort of settlement they would deem just and satisfactory.

There is no good reason why that challenge should not be responded to, and responded to with the utmost candor. We did not wait for it. Not once, but again and again, we have laid our whole thought and purpose before the world, not in general terms only, but each time with sufficient definition to make it clear what sort of definitive terms of settlement must necessarily spring out of them. Within the last week Mr. Lloyd George has spoken with admirable candor and in admirable spirit for the people and government of Great Britain.

There is no confusion of counsel among the adversaries of the Central Powers, no uncertainty of principle, no vagueness of detail. The only secrecy of counsel, the only lack of fearless frankness, the only failure to make definite statements of the objects of the war, lies with Germany and her allies. The issues of life and death hang upon these definitions.

No statesman who has the least conception of his responsibility ought for a moment to permit himself to continue this tragical and appalling outpouring of blood and treasure unless he is sure beyond a peradventure that the objects of the vital sacrifice are part and parcel of the very life of society and that the people for whom he speaks think them right and imperative as he does.

There is, moreover, a voice calling for these definitions of principle and of purpose which is, it seems to me, more thrilling and more compelling than any of the many moving voices with which the troubled air of the world is filled. It is the voice of the Russian people. They are prostrate and all but helpless, it would seem, before the grim power of Germany, which has hitherto known no relenting and no pity. Their power apparently is shattered. And yet their soul is not subservient. They will not yield either in principle or in action. Their conception of what is right, of what is humane and honorable for them to accept, has been stated with a frankness, a largeness of view, a generosity of spirit, and a universal human sympathy which must challenge the admiration of every friend of mankind; and they have refused to compound their ideals or desert others that they themselves may be safe.

They call to us to say what it is that we desire, in what, if in anything, our purpose and our spirit differ from theirs. And I believe that the people of the United States wish us to respond, with utter simplicity and frankness. Whether their present leaders believe it or not, it is our heartfelt desire and hope that some way may be opened whereby we may be permitted to assist the people of Russia to obtain their utmost hope of liberty and ordered peace.

It will be our wish and purpose that the processes of peace, when they are begun, shall be absolutely open and that they shall involve and permit henceforth no secret understandings of any kind. The day of conquest and aggrandizement is gone by; so is also the day of secret covenants entered into in the interest of particular governments and likely at some unlooked-for moment to upset the peace of the world. It is this happy fact, now clear to the view of every public man whose thoughts do not still linger in an age that is dead and gone, which makes it possible for every nation whose purposes are consistent with justice and the peace of the world, to avow now or at any other time the objects it has in view.

We entered this war because violations of right had occurred which touched us to the quick and made the life of our own people impossible unless they were corrected and the world secured once for all against their recurrence. What we demand in this war, therefore, is nothing peculiar to ourselves. It is that the world be made fit and safe to live in, and particularly that it be made safe for every peace-loving nation which, like our own, wishes to live its own life, determine its own institutions, be assured of justice and fair dealing by the other peoples of the world as against force and selfish aggression. All the peoples of the world are in effect partners in this interest, and for our part we see very clearly that unless justice be done to others it will not be done to us.

The program of the world's peace, therefore, is our program; and that program, the only possible program, as we see it, is this:

(1) Open covenants of peace, openly arrived at, after which there shall be no private international understandings of any kind, but diplomacy shall proceed always frankly and in the public view.

(2) Absolute freedom of navigation upon the seas, outside territorial waters, alike in peace and in war, except as the seas may be closed in whole or in part by international action for the enforcement of international covenants.

(3) The removal, so far as possible, of all economic barriers and the establishment of an equality of trade conditions among all the nations consenting to the peace and associating themselves for its maintenance.

(4) Adequate guarantees given and taken that national armaments will be reduced to the lowest point consistent with domestic safety.

(5) A free, open-minded and absolutely impartial

adjustment of all colonial claims, based upon a strict observance of the principle that in determining all such questions of sovereignty the interests of the populations concerned must have equal weight with the equitable claims of the government whose title is to be determined.

(6) The evacuation of all Russian territory and such a settlement of all questions affecting Russia as will secure the best and freest coöperation of the other nations of the world in obtaining for her an unhampered and unembarrassed opportunity for the independent determination of her own political development and national policy and assure her of a sincere welcome into the society of free nations under institutions of her own choosing; and, more than a welcome, assistance also of every kind that she may need and may herself desire. The treatment accorded Russia by her sister nations in the months to come will be the acid test of their good will, of their comprehension of her needs as distinguished from their own interests, and of their intelligent and unselfish sympathy.

(7) Belgium, the whole world will agree, must be evacuated and restored, without any attempt to limit the sovereignty which she enjoys in common with all other free nations. No other single act will serve as this will to restore confidence among the nations in the laws which they have themselves set and demanded for the government of their relations with one another. Without this healing act the whole structure and validity of international law is forever impaired.

(8) All French territory should be freed and the invaded portions restored, and the wrong done to France by Prussia in 1871 in the matter of Alsace-Lorraine, which has unsettled the peace of the world for nearly 50 years, should be righted, in order that peace may once more be made secure in the interest of all.

(9) A readjustment of the frontiers of Italy should be effected along clearly recognizable lines of nationality.

(10) The peoples of Austria-Hungary, whose place among the nations we wish to see safeguarded and assured, should be accorded the freest opportunity of autonomous development.

(11) Roumania, Serbia and Montenegro should be evacuated; occupied territories restored; Serbia accorded free and secure access to the sea; and the relations of the several Balkan states to one another determined by friendly counsel along historically established lines of allegiance and nationality; and international guarantees of the political and economic independence and the territorial integrity of the several Balkan states should be entered into.

(12) The Turkish portions of the present Ottoman empire should be assured a secure sovereignty, but the other nationalities which are now under Turkish rule should be assured an undoubted security of life and an absolutely unmolested opportunity of autonomous development, and the Dardanelles should be permanently opened as a free passage to the ships and commerce of all nations under international guarantees.

(13) An independent Polish state should be erected which should include the territories inhabited by indisputably Polish populations, which should be assured a free and secure access to the sea, and whose political and economic independence and territorial integrity should be guaranteed by international covenant.

(14) A general association of nations must be formed under specific covenants for the purpose of affording mutual guarantees of political independence and territorial integrity to great and small states alike.

In regard to these essential rectifications of wrong and

assertions of right, we feel ourselves to be intimate partners of all the governments and peoples associated together against the imperialists: we cannot be separated in interest or divided in purpose. We stand together until the end.

For such arrangements and covenants we are willing to fight and to continue to fight until they are achieved; but only because we wish the right to prevail and desire a just and stable peace, such as can be secured only by removing the chief provocations to war, which this program does remove. We have no jealousy of German greatness, and there is nothing in this program that impairs it. We grudge her no achievement or distinction of learning or of pacific enterprise such as have made her record very bright and very enviable. We do not wish to injure her or to block in any way her legitimate influence or power. We do not wish to fight her either with arms or with hostile arrangements of trade if she is willing to associate herself with us and the other peace-loving nations of the world in covenants of justice and law and fair dealing. We wish her only to accept a place of equality among the peoples of the world — the new world in which we now live — instead of a place of mastery.

Neither do we presume to suggest to her any alteration or modifications of her institutions. But it is necessary, we must frankly say, and necessary as a preliminary to any intelligent dealings with her on our part, that we should know whom her spokesmen speak for when they speak to us, whether for the Reichstag majority or for the military party and the men whose creed is imperial domination.

We have spoken now, surely in terms too concrete to admit of any further doubt or question. An evident principle runs through the whole program I have outlined.

It is the principle of justice to all peoples and nationalities, and their right to live on equal terms of liberty and safety with one another, whether they be strong or weak. Unless this principle be made its foundation, no part of the structure of international justice can stand. The people of the United States could act upon no other principle, and to the vindication of this principle they are ready to devote their lives, their honor, and everything that they possess. The moral climax of this, the culminating and final war for human liberty, has come, and they are ready to put their own strength, their own highest purpose, their own integrity and devotion to the test.

PRONUNCIATION OF PROPER NAMES

NOTE. — The War has changed many accepted pronunciations, and many foreign sounds do not exist in English. In the following list the sound of French *j* is represented by ż, French *u* by ü, French nasal *m* or *n* by ṅ, and German *ch* by H.

Æschylus (Ĕs′kĭlŭs)

Agrippa (Ȧgrĭp′pä)

Albert Thomas (Älbâr′ Tō′mä)

Alsace (Alsäs′ *or* Alsäs′)

Anatole (Änätôl′)

Annales, les (Ännäl′)

Aristide (Ȧrĭstēd)

Bakhmetieff (Bäkmĕtē′ĕf)

Balfour (Băl′fōōr)

Ballin (Bälēn′)

Balliol (Bä′liol; *also spelled* Baliol)

Bastile (Bästēl′)

Belgia Irredenta (Bĕl′jä Ĭrädĕn′tä)

Bellinzona (Bĕllĭntzō′nä)

Ben Rabinson (Rä′binson)

Berthelot (Bârtạlō′)

Bey (Bā *or* Bē)

Blumenthal (Blōō′mentäl)

Boche (bôsh)

Boer (Bōōr)

Bonar Law (Bŏn′ar)

Boselli, Signor Paolo (sēn′yôr Pou′lō Bŏsĕl′lĭ)

Botzen (Bŏt′sen)

Briand (Brēạṅ′)

Brieg (Brēg)

Brixen (Brĭx′en)

Cadorna (Cadôr′nä)

Camillo (Cämĭl′ō)

Cardiff (Cär′dĭf)

Cavell (Căvĕl′)

Cavour, di (Cävōr′)

ceterum censeo Cartaginem esse delendam (*Latin:* Again I vote that Carthage ought to be wiped out)

Chabannes (Shäbän′)

Chambrun (Shạṅbrŭṅ)

Chasseurs (Shässēr′)

Chiavenna (Kēävĕ′nä)

College St. Barbe (Cŏleż′ Säṅ Bärb)

cuirassiers (Kwērăsiä′)

D'Annunzio (Dänōōn′tzĭō)

de Wiart (de Vēär)

Descartes (Dācärt′)

Deschanel (Dāshänel′)

di Cavour (*see* Cavour)

Djavid Bey (Dyä′vēd Bā)

Dolorosa (*see* Via Dolorosa)

Domo d'Ossola (Dōmō dŏs′sälä)

Doumic (Dōōmēk′)

Doury (Dōōrē′)

dragoons (dragoons′)

Dreyfus (Drā′füs)

Duma (Dū′ma)

Eckstein (Ek′shtīn)

Envers Bey (Ên′vêrs Bā)

Ernst (Ãrnst)

Eviva (Ĕvē′vä)

201

Faubourg St. Antoine (Fō'bōor Sănt Ȧntwän')

fides Teutonica (*Latin:* German faith)

Figaro (Fē'gärō)

Fleurus (Flû'rüs)

Foggia (Fŏg'yä)

Gabriele (Gäbrēēl'ĕ)

Galantuomo (*see* Il Re Galantuomo)

gardes mobiles (gärd mōbēl')

Garibaldi (Gärĭbäl'dĭ)

Giuseppe (Jōosĕp'pĕ)

Gorizia (Gōrēt'zēä)

Göschenen (Gû'shĕnĕn)

grognards (grōnyär')

Hague, the (Häg *or* Hāg)

Haig (Hāg)

Hans (Häns)

Havre (Ȧvr)

Henri (Õṅrē')

Heyman (Hā'män)

Il Re Galantuomo (*Italian:* ēl rä gäläntwō'mō)

Irredenta (Ĭrädĕn'tä)

Italia (Ētä'liä)

Jacques (Żäk)

Jacquet (Żäkä')

Jemappes (Żĕmăp')

Joffre (Żŏf)

Jonescu (Yŏn'ĕshōo)

Kahn (Kän)

Kerensky (Kĕrĕn'skĭ)

Kovno (Kŏv'nō)

Kropotkin (Krōpŏt'kĭn)

Kuhn (Kōōn)

Les Annales (läz ännäl')

Liege (Lēäż')

L'Italia (lētä'liä)

Lissauer (Lĭs'ouĕr)

Llanystymdwy (*Welsh:* Unpronounceable by any but natives)

Loeb (Lōb)

Loire (Lwär)

Lorraine (Lō rän')

Louvain (Loovăṅ')

Maeterlinck (Mạ'terlink)

Magyar (Măg'yär)

Mahomet (Ma hom'et; *also* spelled Mohammed)

Maurice (Mōrēs' *or* Mŏr'ris)

Mazzini (Mätzē'nĭ)

Mercier (Märsiä')

Meyer (Mī'ĕr)

Molière (Mōliär')

Moncheur (Mŏṅshûr')

Monsieur (mēsyē')

Nairobi (Nī ro'bi, capital of a British province in the East African Protectorate)

Nivelle (Nēvĕl')

Oësterreich (Ēstĕrrīн. German name for Austria)

Palmerston (Päm'erston)

Paolo Boselli (Poulō Bŏsĕl'lĭ)

Pascal (Päscäl')

Pasteur (Pästĕr')

Pescara (Päscä'rä)

Petain (Pĕtăṅ')

Petit Parisien (Pĕtē' Pärĭzĭäṅ')

Plataea (Pla tē'ạ)

Pleiades (Plē'ạ dēz)

Poincare (Pwăṅcärä')

Prato (Prä'tō)

Premier (Prĕmĭä' *or* prĕmēr')

Premiership (prĭmēr'ship)

Rabelais (Räbēlä′)
Rabinson, Ben (Rä′binson)
Re (*see* Il Re Galantuomo)
Reichshofen (Rīhs′hōfĕn)
Reichstag (Rīhs′täн)
Renan (Rēnáṅ′)
René (Rēnä′)
Revue (Rĕvü′)
Rheims (Rāṅs)
Rhodesia (Rōdē′sĭạ *or* Rōdē′zĭạ)
Ribot (Rēbō′)
Ritter Tannhäuser (Rĭt′tĕr Tän′-
    hoysĕr)
Rochambeau (Rōshạṅbō′)
Rodzianko (Rŏdzïän′kō)
Rothschild (Rōt′shĭld)

Saint, *see* St. (*French* Săṅ)
Salamis (Săl′ạmĭs)
Salandra (Sälän′drä)
sang-froid (sạṅ′frwä)
Saverne (Sävärn′)
Schleswig (Shläs′vĭg)
Schweiz (Shvītz, German name
    for Switzerland)
Seine (Sān)
Somme (Sȯm)
Sonnino (Sȯnē′nō)
Sorbonne (Sȯrbȯn′)
Spielmann (Shpēlmän)
St. Antoine, *see* Faubourg
St. Barbe, *see* College
St. Ives (Săṅtēv′ *or* Saint Ives)
St. Louis (Săṅlōōē *or* Saint Lewis)
St. Moritz (Saint Mạ′ritz, a
    Swiss winter resort)
St. Vincent de Paul (Săṅ Vănsȯṅ′
    dĕ Pōl)
status quo ante (*Latin:* previous
    situation)

status quo ante bellum (*Latin:*
    situation before the war)
Styr (Stēr)

Taine (Tān)
Take Jonescu (Täkä Yŏn′ĕshōō)
Tannhäuser (Tän′hoysĕr)
Tedeschi (Tĕdĕs′kĭ)
Teutonia (Toytō′nĭä *or* Tōōtō′nĭä)
Teutonica fides (Toytō′nĭcä fēdäs,
    Latin: Teuton or German
    faith)
Thibault (Tēbō′)
Thomas, Albert (Tō′mä, Älbâr)
Tolstoi (Tôl′stoy)
Troia (Troy′ä)
Tsing-tao (Tsĭng-tou)
Tyrol (Tўr′ol)

Udine (ōōd′inĕ *or* oodē′nĕ)

Valmy (Väl′mĭ)
Verdun (Värdŭṅ′)
Via Dolorosa (vē′ä *or* wē ä
    dōlōrō′sä)
Vistula (Vis′tū lä)
Viviani (Vĭvĭä′nĭ)
Voituret (Vwätürä′)
Voltaire (Vạltär′)
Vosges (Vōż)

Walhalla (Välhäl′lä) (mythical
    palace of immortality for those
    slain in battle)
Wiart, *see* de Wiart

Yser (Ēzēr)

Zangwill (Zäng′wĭll)
Zinsser (Tzĭn′zēr)
Zouaves (Zōōäv′)

INDEX OF AUTHORS

Effective English

By P. P. CLAXTON, United States Commissioner of Education, and JAMES MCGINNISS, Principal of the High School, Ludlow, Kentucky, 12mo, cloth, 584 pages. Price, $1.25.

EFFECTIVE ENGLISH is a complete text-book in rhetoric covering every phase of secondary English.

Realizing the importance of enthusiasm in the work in English the authors have set out to secure the pupils' interest at the start and to hold it to the end. The variety, vigor, and definiteness of the presentation will attract young pupils.

The book is distinctly literary in character; quotations from the best writers abound in its pages. The authors hold that the most practical English is learned from the best models. In choosing these models preference has been given to those which have permanent literary value. Special attention is given, and frequent references are made, to the great folk-epics of the Greeks, Germans, and Northmen.

Over half the book is devoted to practice. Every rule and principle is carefully illustrated, and ample drill is afforded to fix it in the pupil's mind.

The exercises cover the whole range of school activity from the interests of classical schools with their emphasis on Latin and Greek traditions to the commercial school with its stress upon Business English. There are exercises adapted to every variety of boy and girl, whether they are interested in art, bird-lore, pageantry, or the " movies."

The book is illustrated with handsome half-tones, which are made the basis of work in composition.

Effective English is divided into six parts, thoroughly discussing all forms from the elements of effective speaking and writing to the finer points of effective style and criticism. Part VI treats of Grammar.

The Appendix deals with Preparation of Manuscript, Punctuation and Capitalization, and Suggestions to Teachers.

Paragraph-Writing

By F. N. SCOTT, Professor of Rhetoric in the University of Michigan, and J. V. DENNEY, Professor of English in Ohio State University. Revised edition. 12mo, cloth, 480 pages. Price, $1.25.

FOR this new edition the book has been entirely rewritten and much enlarged. The fundamental idea of the book is, as before, to treat the paragraph as the unit of composition; in adapting the work, however, to the present needs of college and university classes many modifications in general plan and in detail have been made. Among these changes may be mentioned the following: —

The book has been enlarged so as to include the various types of composition — that is, Description, Narration, Exposition, and Argument. These are treated at length and with a thoroughness corresponding to their present importance in college work.

The exercises for individual work have been removed from the text and placed in a division by themselves. This arrangement lends continuity to the text and at the same time gives space for a greatly extended series of progressive exercises offering a wide choice to instructor and student.

The illustrative matter of the preceding edition, through long use somewhat familiar to both teacher and student, has been replaced by fresh and worthy material from a great variety of sources. In amount this material has been more than doubled.

American Literature with Readings

By ROY BENNETT PACE, Assistant Professor of English in Swarthmore College, Swarthmore, Pennsylvania. 12mo, cloth, 671 pages. Price, $1.35.

THIS book is the author's American Literature and Readings in American Literature bound together in one volume. With it in the hands of the pupil, teachers are able to carry out, at no great expense, the author's plan of studying the various writers with their works in accessible form.

Orations and Arguments

Edited by C. B. BRADLEY, Professor of Rhetoric in the University of California. 12mo, cloth, 385 pages. Price, $1.00.

The following speeches are contained in the book : —

BURKE:
On Conciliation with the Colonies, and Speech before the Electors at Bristol.

CHATHAM:
On American Affairs.

ERSKINE:
In the Stockdale Case.

LINCOLN:
The Gettysburg Address.

WEBSTER:
The Reply to Hayne.

MACAULAY
On the Reform Bill of 1832.

CALHOUN:
On the Slavery Question.

SEWARD:
On the Irrepressible Conflict.

IN making this selection, the test applied to each speech was that it should be in itself memorable, attaining its distinction through the essential qualities of nobility and force of ideas, and that it should be, in topic, so related to the great thoughts, memories, or problems of our own time as to have for us still an inherent and vital interest.

The Notes aim to furnish the reader with whatever help is necessary to the proper appreciation of the speeches ; to avoid bewildering him with mere subtleties and display of erudition ; and to encourage in him habits of self-help and familiarity with sources of information.

Note-taking

By S. S. SEWARD, Jr., Assistant Professor of English in the Leland Stanford Junior University. 12mo, flexible cloth, 91 pages. Price, 50 cents.

THIS book is the result of a number of years' experience in training students to take notes intelligently and systematically, and has been written with the conviction that a better standard of note-taking will add much to the effectiveness of the students' work.

It contains chapters on The Aim in Note-taking, How to Condense Notes, How to Organize Notes, Special Problems in Notetaking, together with exercises for practice and many examples.

Public Speaking: A Treatise on Delivery with Selections for Declaiming

By EDWIN D. SHURTER, Associate Professor of Oratory in the University of Texas. 12mo, cloth, 265 pages. Price, 90 cents.

THIS book treats chiefly of persuasive speaking, and the author lays stress on the fact that mental qualities, such as clearness, simplicity, vivacity, spontaneity, and sincerity, are of chief value in declamation. Although this principle is counted fundamental, the book has all the necessary rules and principles for the technique of public speaking, with exercises for perfecting the voice and for overcoming defects of speech. Gesture is treated in a very happy way, as the physical expression of earnestness.

The chapters are : —

I. The Nature and Basis of Public Speaking.
II. The Voice.
III. Pronunciation and Enunciation.
IV. Key.
V. Emphasis.
VI. Inflection.
VII. Time: Phrasing, Transition.
VIII. Force, Climax, Volume.
IX. Tone-Color.
X. Earnestness.
XI. Physical Earnestness — Gesture.
XII. General Suggestions.
XIII. Selections for Practice.

The Selections for Practice include speeches from Lincoln, Roosevelt, Blaine, Grady, John Hay, Woodrow Wilson, Wendell Phillips, Henry Watterson, and many others.

A Drill Book in English

Compiled by GEORGE E. GAY, Haverhill, Mass. 12mo, cloth, 108 pages. Price, 45 cents.

THIS manual will appeal only to teachers who believe that there is value in presenting to the pupils specimens of bad English for correction. It contains in brief form rules for spelling, punctuation, capitalization, and the most important principles of grammar and rhetoric. Abundant exercises for practice are given.